THE STATE AND VARNA FORMATION IN THE MID-GANGA PLAINS

An Ethnoarchaeological View

THE STATE AND VARNA FORMATION IN THE MID-GANGA PLAINS

An Ethnoarchaeological View

RAM SHARAN SHARMA

Sharda Memorial Lecture

SHARDA MEMORIAL EDUCATIONAL TRUST
VARANASI

MANOHAR
2017

First published 1996
Reprinted 2001, 2017

ISBN 978-81-7304-169-3

Published by
Ajay Kumar Jain *for*
Manohar Publishers & Distributors
4753/23 Ansari Road, Daryaganj
New Delhi 110 002

Printed at
Shri Ganpati Enterprises
Delhi 110 052

Contents

List of Illustrations

Acknowledgements

The book has grown out of the Sharda Memorial Lecture I delivered at Banaras Hindu University in 1995. I am grateful to Dr Shanta, Professor Hira Lal Singh and Dr Anand Shankar Singh for inviting me to give the lecture. In preparing the copy for publication I have received help from Professor K.M. Shrimali and Shyam Narayan Lal of the University of Delhi and Dr Arundhati Banerjee of the Archaeological Survey of India. Professor Purushottam Singh, Dr Birendra Pratap Singh and Dr Vibha Tripathi of Banaras Hindu University have been kind enough to show me the antiquities and the unpublished material relating to my area of study. I have received similar help from my friends at Patna Dr Anjani

Kumar, A.K. Prasad, Dr Basudev Narayan, Dr S.R. Roy and Dr B.S. Verma. I sincerely acknowledge the contributions of all these scholars towards the completion of this book and wish to thank them all.

Patna
1 May 1996

R. S. SHARMA

Abbreviations

AŚ	*Arthaśāstra of Kauṭilya*
ASI	Archaeological Survey of India
AV	*Atharva Veda*
BHU	Banaras Hindu University
EIA	*An Encyclopaedia of Indian Archaeology*
IAR	*Indian Archaeology—A Review*
JASB	*Journal of the Asiatic Society of Bengal*
NBPW	Northern Black Polished Ware
PB	*Pañcaviṃśa Brāhmaṇa*
PGW	Painted Grey Ware
PTS	Pali Text Society
RV	*Ṛg Veda*
VI	*Vedic Index of Names and Subjects*

CHAPTER 1

Notions of the State and Varna Society

The Kauṭilyan Structure of the State

It is remarkable that in spite of centuries of progress and change, Kauṭilya's concept of state has stood the test of time. According to Kauṭilya, the state comprises seven elements, namely the sovereign head (*svāmin*), minister (*amātya*), populated territory (*janapada*), fort (*durga*), treasury (*kośa*), coercive power (*daṇḍa*) and friend (*mitra*).[1] This ancient view of the state broadly covers its modern constituents, which include sovereignty, government or bureaucracy, territory and population. Although Kauṭilya attaches the greatest importance to *kośa*[2] and says that force (*daṇḍa*) arises out of treasury (*kośa*), he does not ignore the other elements of the state.[3] On the other hand, the Buddhist school, which propounded the contract theory of the origin of the state, considers taxes to be the only distinctive feature of the state. The *Suttanipāta,* the earliest Pali text, states: 'And whosoever among men gets his rents from village or a populated territory (*raṭṭañ*) know this, O Vaseṭṭha, is a king and no brahmana'.[4]

Claessen on Traits of the Early State

Kauṭilya's concept of the state may be compared with the traits of the early state postulated by Claessen. Claessen expounds seven traits.

(1) The state has a population sufficient to make possible social categorisation, social stratification and specialisation. (2) Its citizenship is determined by residence or birth in the territory, which according to us means that citizenship is not defined by membership of a clan or a tribe. (3) The government has centralised control and possesses the necessary power to maintain law and order through the use of both force and authority. (4) The state is independent at least in fact, and the government has sufficient power to prevent separation and the capacity to meet external threats. (5) The population shows enough of stratification which enables us to distinguish between the emergent social classes of the ruler and the ruled. (6) Productivity is high enough to ensure regular surplus which is used for the maintenance of the state organisation. (7) The state has a common ideology on which the legitimacy of the ruling stratum is based.[5] It will appear that several of these structural traits including population, territory, differentiation in the population, central control, force and surplus leading to taxes are common to the ancient Indian definition. On the other hand fort, high functionaries and ally do not appear

in Claessen's traits of the early state. Though there is no place for ideology in the Indian definition, the aims and ideals to be followed by the king are often stated.

Claessen's definition can work as a basis for our inquiry. Some of the structural and functional traits of the early state postulated by him and ancient Indian thinkers may be considered necessary conditions for its genesis. These are specialisation, social stratification, high productivity and use of force. These traits can be inferred from the archaeological finds. Through the study of artefacts we can look for both craft specialisation and social stratification. An examination of cutting, digging and other production tools together with that of the soil and the material on which the people worked can give us an idea of the nature and extent of productivity. Finally, an analysis of forts and weapons could enlighten us about the use of force. Although much remains to be done in the archaeology of the mid-Ganga plains the existing material can be used for our investigation.

Concept of the Complex Society

The appearance of the state is interlinked with the presence of complex society. Anthropologists believe that the earliest societies were basically kin-based and egalitarian and hence 'simple societies' headed by band leaders or chiefs. In contrast, the complex society was a state-based society, marked by stratification, and its members were differentiated from one another on the basis of birth, status and above all resources. This kind of social stratification distinguishes the varna-divided society found in the age of the Buddha in the mid-Ganga plains. The rules laid down in the earliest law-books called the Dharmasūtras discriminate between the four varnas not only socially, but also politically, economically and religiously. Members of lower orders or varnas cannot take wives from higher orders,[6] and those from the sudra varna cannot be appointed to high posts in the government.[7] Laws of inheritance discriminate against the issues of the brahmanas from lower varna women,[8] and the higher is the varna the lower is the rate of interest.[9] The sudras are not allowed to perform sacrifice and learn the Vedas, and they also suffer from many other disabilities.[10]

The provisions laid down in the Dharmasūtras cannot be dismissed as merely normative. The Buddhist texts clearly show the protest of Gautama Buddha against social stratification based on birth, and the Buddhist dialogues leave no doubt that social hierarchy was a stark reality. This impression is also gathered from the Aśokan inscriptions, the account of Megasthenes and early Prakrit texts. While explaining the term *janapada,* Kauṭilya provides that the territory should be populated by members of the lower orders (*avaravarṇaprāya*) who are capable of paying taxes and supplying labour power.[11] Thus, the *Arthaśāstra* and other texts confirm the existence of privileged interest groups in the form of the two higher orders or varnas dominating the tax-paying and labour-supplying groups identical with vaiśyas and sudras. Therefore, besides the protection of patriarchal family and private property, an important function assigned to the king or the head of the state is the preservation of the varna-divided society. It is his function to see that members of every varna perform the duties allotted to them. It has been shown elsewhere that the state originates because of social differentiation,[12] and once differentiation appears the state upholds it.

Beginnings of Political History in the Mid-Ganga Plains

The political history of the mid-Ganga plains in the pre-600 BC period comprising ancient Kasi, Kosala, Videha, Vaishali,

Magadha and Anga has been reconstructed in great detail by the erudite historian Hemchandra Raychaudhuri. Depending heavily on Vedic sources supplemented by the Puranic genealogy,[13] he does not accept the Puranic list of regnal years, which covers more than 1600 years before Aśoka's coronation according to the figures given for Magadha.[14] His work is a great improvement on F.G. Pargiter's, who relies mainly on the Puranic legends and genealogies and takes back the dynastic history of Magadha to 1300 BC.[15] Utilising epic and Puranic material several scholars have written the history of Kosala, Videha and Vaishali,[16] and if their argument is accepted, the origin of the state system in the mid-Ganga basin can be traced back to 1500 BC or even earlier. However, the picture of the political and administrative system prevalent in the upper and mid-Ganga plains presented by Raychaudhuri (on the basis of later Vedic texts) in the pre-600 BC period cannot be pushed back to 1500 BC. But other writings suggest the domination of the brahmanas in the mid-Ganga basin even in *c.*1500 BC; they also suggest that the kṣatriyas also played an important role. The dominance of the two upper orders presupposes the general subjection of the vaiśyas and sudras.

But the crucial question is: does the material culture revealed by archaeology warrant the presence of the state and social stratification in pre-fifth century BC times in the mid-Ganga plains? Do we notice sufficiently high productivity and a good many settlements leading to the rise of the state and stratified society around 1500 BC or even 1000 BC? To answer these questions one needs to examine the cultural equipment of the people of the alluvial plains in the neolithic and chalcolithic ages and to understand the nature and extent of their interaction with those from the upper Gangetic plains and elsewhere. Developments in other parts of the country also deserve attention.

NOTES

1. R. P. Kangle, ed. & tr., *The Kauṭilīya Arthaśāstra*, University of Bombay, vol. 1 (abbreviated as *AŚ*), VI.1.
2. *AŚ.* VIII. 1.
3. R.S. Sharma, *Aspects of Political Ideas and Institutions in Ancient India*, 3rd edn, Motilal Banarsidass, Delhi, 1991, pp. 32-7.
4. Ibid., pp. 37-8 with fn. 1 on p. 38.
5. Henri J.M. Claessen and Peter Skalnik, eds., *The Early State*, Mouton Publishers, The Hague, 1978, p. 586-9.
6. R.S. Sharma, *Perspectives in Social and Economic History of Early India*, 2nd edn, Munshiram Manoharlal, New Delhi, 1995, pp. 49-60.
7. Sharma, *Aspects of Political Ideas and Institutions in Ancient India*, ch. XVI.
8. R.S. Sharma, *Some Economic Aspects of the Caste System in Ancient India*, Patna, 1952.
9. Ibid.
10. R.S. Sharma, *Śūdras in Ancient India*, 3rd edn, Motilal Banarsidass, Delhi, 1990, ch. IV.
11. *AŚ*, II. I.
12. R.S. Sharma, *Origin of the State in India*, Department of History, University of Bombay, Bombay, 1989.
13. H.C. Raychaudhuri, *Political History of Ancient India*, 7th edn, University of Calcutta, Calcutta, 1972.
14. Heinrich von Stietencron in Heinz Bechert, ed., *When did the Buddha Live?*, Sri Satguru Publications, Delhi, 1995, p. 228.
15. *Ancient Indian Historical Tradition*, London, 1922.
16. Yogendra Mishra, *An Early History of Vaiśālī*, Motilal Banarsidass, Delhi, 1962.

CHAPTER 2

Ecological Setting[1]

Plain Area and Hilly Projections

The mid-Ganga plains cover an area of approximately 160,000 sq. km extending from the confluence of the Ganga and the Yamuna at Allahabad in the west to Rajmahal in the east where the Ganga takes a turn to the south. From the foothills of the Himalaya in the north to the spurs of the Vindhya range and Chotanagpur plateau in the south, the width of this plain extends about 100 km on an average. The outcroppings of the south Bihar plateau are found even in the plains as in the case of the Kharagpur hills near Munger and Patharghata near Kahalgaon in Bhagalpur district. The Rajgir hills in Nalanda district and the Barabar hills near Gaya are well known. The hills bordering the plains together with their outcrops inside are sources of stone and metals. The south Bihar plateau is rich in copper and also in iron ores of high quality, which may have been used by the state of Magadha. Kosala may have used the iron ores of Banda district in Uttar Pradesh, and Kasi that of eastern Madhya Pradesh. The southern part of the mid-Ganga plains was conveniently located, vis-a-vis the iron mines in Singhbhum, Mayurbhanj and Keonjhar on the south-east, and eastern Madhya Pradesh in the west-south. The distribution of copper-hoards in Ranchi, Hazaribagh and Palamau suggests that both the sources of iron and copper could be reached by land routes, though the Son river may have given access to eastern Madhya Pradesh.

Sometimes the role of paleolithic, mesolithic and megalithic sites is exaggerated in what is known as the 'Ganga Valley'.[2] The various sites of stone age found in this area are connected with the Vindhya ranges or the Chotanagpur plateau. Some such sites are also found in the Meja subdivision of Allahabad district and in the Chandauli subdivision of Varanasi. Further, a good number of mesolithic sites, which were witnesses to the scenes of seasonal migration of people from the Vindhyan ranges, appear in Pratapgarh district. Numerous graves of mesolithic people, who lived basically by hunting and gathering, are located in this district near horse-shoe shaped lakes. They seem to belong to *c.* 9000 BC. The stone age settlement in these areas really belong to the spurs of the Vindhyan mountains. This is also true of the paleolithic settlement found in Paisra village in Munger and neolithic settlements in Senuwar in Rohtas district. The legacy of the paleolithic, mesolithic, neolithic and the megalithic settlers contributed to the development of material life in the pre-NBPW and later phases, although much cannot be made of the megaliths which appeared after *c.* 500 BC.

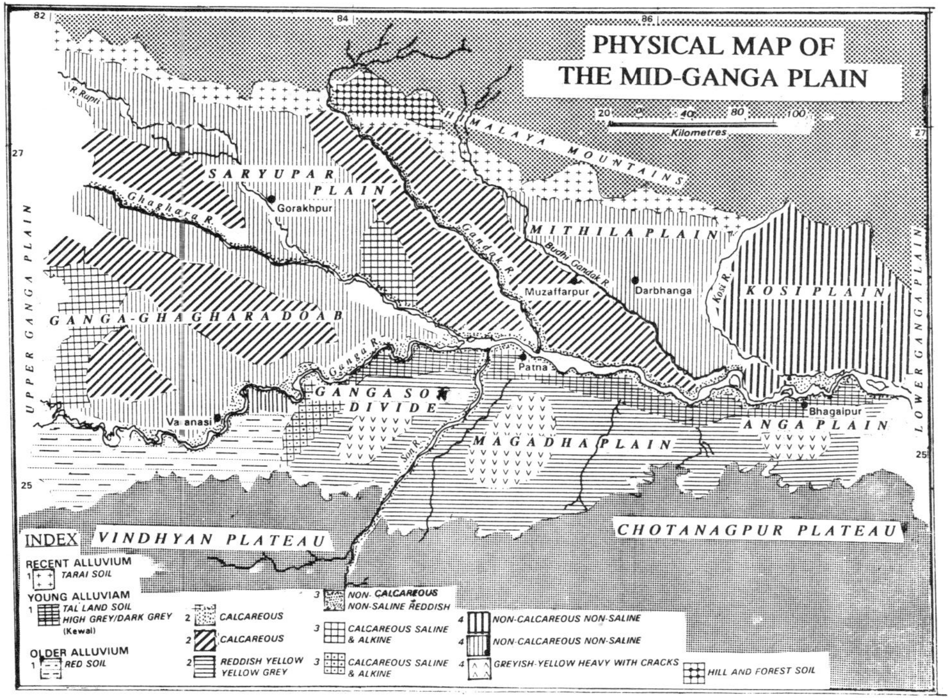

MAP 1: PHYSICAL MAP OF MID-GANGA PLAIN

Water-logged Areas

It seems that from 10000 BC onwards, when the Holocene period set in, humid conditions set in in the mid-Ganga plains. It is held that there have been no fundamental changes in climatic conditions since 9000 BC. Humid conditions caused by the heavy monsoon rains created in the plains two important phenomena: forests and lakes or water-logged lands. Most studies have taken into account only two types of terrain, the hilly areas and river banks. But the water-logged areas are equally important. Lakes, called *chars* in the dialects of north Bihar, were formed in the plains of eastern U.P. and north Bihar by the shifting river courses. But unless the depth of the silt deposited in the lake areas is measured scientifically the exact age of present water-logged areas cannot be determined. However, those found in the Kosi zone, where geochronologically this river is very active, may have been of recent origin. Nevertheless in the areas, in which the beds of the rivers such as those of the Gandak and Ganga are more or less fixed within a certain range, lake formations, large or small, may have existed from early times. As early as 5000 BC nearly 200 seasonal mesolithic camps appear on the banks of the lakes in Pratapgarh district and its neighbourhood in eastern U.P. It is easier to settle on the boundaries of the lakes where problems of clearance may not have been as difficult as in the lake-free forest area. Further, the lakes offered various types of food not found either in the running water or the rivers.

Some lakes certainly existed in chalcolithic times around 1200 BC, as can be inferred from numerous shells found in Narhan located on the bank of a lake in Gorakhpur district. Ancient settlements founded on the banks of the Ganga, Gandak, Saryu and Rapti rivers are well known, but settlements situated on the banks of the lakes still have to be studied in depth. Rampurba, Lauriya-Nandangarh and Areraj, where Asokan pillars have been found, are located close to the *char.* Similar is the case with Pandavgarh and Mangalgarh in Samastipur district and Jaymangalagarh in Begusarai district; at all these sites NBPW shards appear on the surface. Jayamangalagarh is situated on the bank of the Kabar lake which is 12 km long and 3 km wide.[3] In Muzaffarpur district, Katragarh, which shows settlement in the third century BC, is situated on the Joga Nala, an old bed of the Bagmati.[4] These instances may indicate that the earliest settlements in the alluvial tracts appeared not only on the river banks, but also near the lakes.

Soil, Rainfall, Humidity and Vegetation

The alluvial soil found in the water-logged areas was very fertile. But it was as difficult to break it as the *kewal* or the calcareous soil south of the Ganga; the term *kewal* is also used in some parts of north Bihar. Tillage could not be carried on either effectively or extensively either with wooden ploughshares or with microliths. Only iron shares could serve this purpose in the *char* areas, where the hardness of soil is indicated by the local adjectives *chikaṭ, sakkat* and *kumbhrauṭī* applied to it.

The mid-Ganga plains can be clearly demarcated on several grounds. The middle plains get far more rainfall and humidity than the upper Ganga plains. The average rainfall in this area varies from about 1600 mm to 1000 mm. This naturally gives rise to thick vegetation, and the trees in this area have thick stems. The general slope of the Ganga is from north-west to south-east, but from Allahabad onwards the river enters flat plains which contain several areas which often get flooded. The slope from the north to the south is invariably more fertile than the north. Further, the mid-Ganga plains possess new alluvium in contrast to the old alluvium which is found in the upper Gangetic plains. A continuous process of silt deposit has made certain portions of the mid-Ganga plains, especially in the districts of Patna and Gaya, extremely clayey. The clayey soil is also found in the plains north of the Ganga in eastern U.P. and also in north Bihar. As mentioned earlier, old alluvium is easier to break whereas clayey soil is not. It can retain moisture for a longer duration which leads to the corrosion of antiquities including iron implements that form a part of habitational deposits in this area. Consequently, the survival rate of iron objects in this area is low. They are far better preserved in the dry and semi-arid zone. Those found at Atranjikhera in western U.P. and Noh in Rajasthan are in a better shape. Iron objects found in excavations at Pataliputra are so corroded that none of them is considered fit for reproduction by the excavator. Antiquities are preserved better in the loamy and sandy soil which appears in Champa and Maner in Bihar, and also in Narhan in eastern U.P.

The mid-Ganga plains had a thick vegetation cover on account of heavy rainfall. Settlement on the plains was not possible without clearance which was more difficult in the clayey area and less in the loamy and sandy area. The sandy and the loamy soil of the tarai area in the foothills of the Himalaya facilitated a few early historical settlements such as Tilauarakot in Nepal and Piparahwa and Ganwaria in eastern Uttar Pradesh; the same factor helped settlements in Sonpur and Taradih in Gaya district.

NOTES

1. This section is mainly based on O.H.K. Spate and A.T.A. Learmonth, *India and Pakistan: A General and Regional Geography*, Methuen & Co. Ltd, London, 1967, pp. 563-70, and on my own field-work.

2. A balanced study of the Stone Age cultures appears in Basudev Narayan, *Prehistoric Archaeology of Bihar*, K.P. Jayaswal Research Institute, Patna, 1996:
3. D.R. Patil, *Antiquarian Remains in Bihar*, K. P. Jayaswal Research Institute, Patna, 1961, p. 191.
4. Ibid., p. 196.

CHAPTER 3

Neolithic-Chalcolithic Background

Settlement

Stone age settlements were possible in areas adjacent to the hills, lakes and river confluences. Tools found in Paisera village near Kharagpur hills in Munger[1] and also in the Belan valley on the spurs of the Vindhyas in Allahabad district indicate the presence of the paleolithic people on the fringes of the Gangetic plains. Mesolithic relics of about 9000 BC appear in Pratapgarh district.[2] The earliest neolithic settlement in the plain appears in Chirand around 2000 BC, and merges with the chalcolithic layers. But settlements in the stone age cannot be a general feature of the plains because of the difficulty of obtaining stone. The neolithic-chalcolithic complexes in Chirand, Chechar-Kutubpur and

Maner lie in the interior of the mid-Ganga basin. They appear on the confluence of the Ganga, Son, Gandak and Ghaghra on loamy and sandy soil where clearance was facilitated by floods. Similarly, the neolithic and chalcolithic complexes at Sohgaura[3] are located near the confluence of the Rapti and Ami rivers. In all such places lithic tools are not found in large numbers. Microliths appear in the form of blades and seem to be of little use in food production. Antlers and other bone tools appear in profusion. The neolithic-chalcolithic complexes in Taradih and Senuwar, and the chalcolithic site in Sonpur, are situated in the hilly areas. Significantly enough the earliest settlements at Taradih and Sonpur appear on sandy soil,[4] which precludes thick vegetation. In Oriup in Bhagalpur district the chalcolithic site is close to the Patharghata hills near Kahalgaon.

Tools and Craft Specialisation

Stone and bone tools were more important than copper tools in the mid-Ganga plains during the neolithic and chalcolithic phases. The chalcolithic phase has so little of copper and so much of bone and stone that it is perhaps more appropriate to refer to it as osteolithic. However, in Chirand, antlers and bone tools outnumber stone tools. Bone points and arrowheads abound in Champa,[5] Sonpur,[6] Maner,[7] Taradih,[8] Khairadih[9] and Narhan.[10] The find of bone objects and styluses in NBPW levels shows[11] that the use of bone continued even after the introduction of iron tools. Many bone objects appear at Pataliputra, Prahladpur and Taradih in the NBPW phase;[12] numerous finished and unfinished bone tools belong to the early phase of NPBW at Manjhi.[13] In neolithic-chalcolithic times bone tools were largely used for hunting and very little for digging. Stone tools could not be easily transported to the alluvial plains.

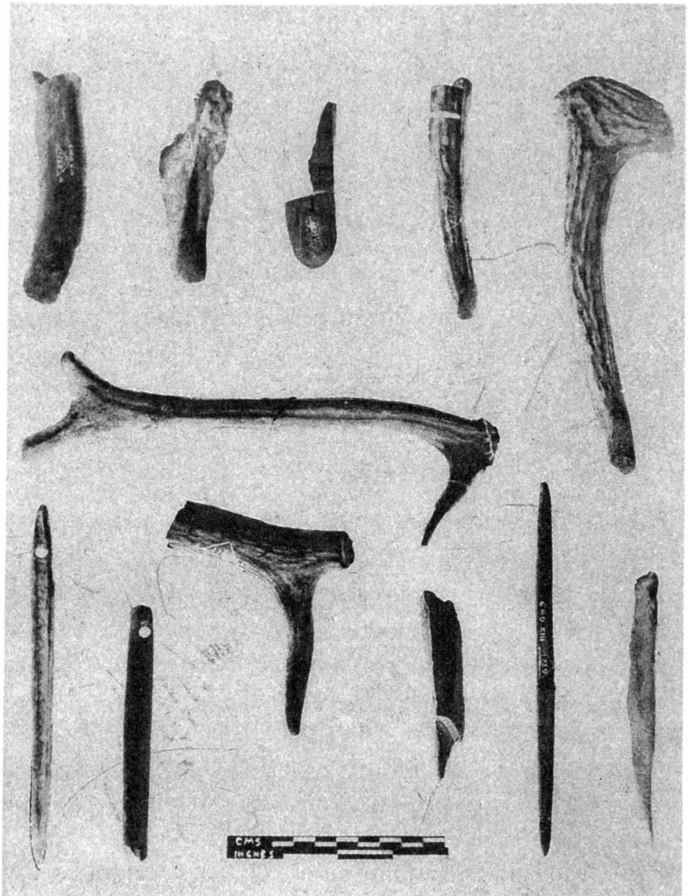

PLATE 1: CUTTING, DIGGING AND WEEDING TOOLS FROM NEOLITHIC CHIRAND

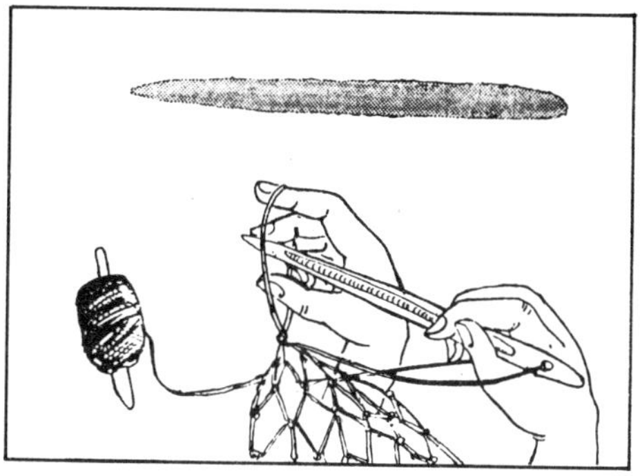

Bodokin—a net knitting tool

Process of net knitting

FIGURE 1: ETHNOLOGICAL PROJECTIONS OF THE USE OF THE BODOKIN FROM NEOLITHIC CHIRAND

But it was easier to hunt deer and other animals for food and prepare tools out of their horns and bones.

Copper tools of the chalcolithic phase are very few in Narhan and Prahaladpur and also in Maner and Taradih. Copper objects mainly comprise arrowheads and antimony rods. Though more effective than bone and stone in digging, copper tools are scarcely found in excavations. The chalcolithic people of the mid-Ganga plains did not know of bronze tools and yet they had perfected the art of socketing. Khairadih shows a socketed arrowhead of bone and a socketed arrowhead of copper.[14] The knowledge that socketing was perhaps better than hafting may have prepared the way for the socketing of the iron share into the wooden plough in NBPW times.

Beginning of Cereal Cultivation

The pre-NBPW people were certainly food producing, and remains of foodgrains discovered are a pointer to the neolithic-chalcolithic phase. Rice from Koldihwa is dated to 5000 BC though it may belong to *c.* 1500 BC. However, in pre-NBPW times rice appears in Chirand, Taradih, Sonpur, Narhan and several other places. The neolithic phase of Taradih shows rice, barley, lentil, black pea, gram and millets, while its chalcolithic phase adds green gram and chick pea to these cereals.[15] In the pre-1000 BC period the people of Imlidih-Khurd in Gorakhpur district, who used copper and cord impressed red ware, produced rice, wheat, barley, jowar and pearl-millet in addition to lentil, green gram, field-pea and grass-pea. Their oil seeds included sesame (*tila*).[16] In *c.* tenth-eighth centuries BC Narhan shows rice, barley, three forms of wheat, pea, green gram, chick pea, sesame and *khesārī* (*Lethyrus sativus*). Seeds of mustard and flax or *alsi* suggest wild seed crops. The jackfruit was also known. Rice, barley, pea and green gram appear again between 800 and 600 BC.[17] One Narhan trench shows the use of cultivated rice, barley, bread-wheat, black gram, gram, pea, *khesārī*, *kodo*, millet and sesame in 500-400 BC.[18] It is argued that most cereals came to the mid-Ganga plains from the Harappan culture in the second millennium BC,[19] but this cannot be accepted unless intermediate sites with Harappan assemblages are discovered.

Desertion and Continuity of Chalcolithic Sites

Unlike the chalcolithic sites in western and central India those in the mid-Ganga plains were not deserted. More than a dozen chalcolithic sites in western and central India show a sudden break in culture. They were deserted for 500 to 1000 years and reoccupied between the fifth and the third century BC. These include Ahar[20] and Gilund[21] in Rajasthan; Jokha,[22] Dhatva[23] and Prabhaspatan[24] in Gujarat; Besnagar,[25] Kayatha,[26] Maheshwar and Navdatoli[27] in Madhya Pradesh, and finally Jorwe,[28] Nasik,[29] Nevasa,[30] Bahal[31] and Songaon[32] in Maharashtra. Possibly the non-availability of iron and its technology ruled out any expansion of the old settlements after the exhaustion of the fertility of the local soil. People did not face this difficulty in the mid-Ganga basin where several chalcolithic settlements grew into full-fledged iron age settlements.

NOTES

1. *IAR 1983-84*, pp. 13-14.
2. Kenneth A.R. Kennedy *et al.*, 'Mesolithic Human Remains from the Gangetic Plain: Sarai Nehar Rai', *Puratattva*, no. 15, 1984-5, pp. 1-55.
3. S.N. Chaturvedi, 'Advance of Vindhyan Neolithic and Chalcolithic Cultures to the Himalyan Terai', in *Man and Environment*, IX, 1985, p. 103.
4. B.P. Sinha and B.S. Verma, *Sonpur Excavations (1956 and 1959-*

62), Directorate of Archaeology and Museums, Bihar, Patna, 1977, p. 18.
5. *IAR 1982-83*, pp. 15-16.
6. B.P. Sinha and B.S. Verma, *Sonpur Excavations*, pp. 18, 130
7. *IAR 1985-86*, p. 11.
8. *IAR 1983-84*, p. 12; 1984-5, p. 10; 1985-6, p. 8.
9. *IAR 1982-83*, p. 93.
10. *IAR 1985-86*, p. 81.
11. *IAR 1982-83*, p. 16.
12. B.P. Sinha and L.A. Narain, *Pataliputra Excavations_1955-56*, Directorate of Archaeology and Museums, Bihar, Patna, 1970, p. 55; A.K. Narain and T.N. Roy, *The Excavations at Prahladpur, March-April 1963*, Banaras Hindu University, Varanasi, 1968, pp. 38-39.
13. *IAR 1983-84*, p. 16.
14. *IAR 1982-83*, pp. 92-3, also see plate no. 56.
15. Information from A.K. Prasad.
16. K.S. Saraswat, 'Seed and Fruit Remains of Imlidih-Khurd, Gorakhpur: A Preliminary Report', in *Prāgdhārā*, no. 3 (1993), pp. 37-41.
17. *IAR 1985-86*, p. 123. Revised radiocarbon dates appear in Purushottam Singh, *Excavations at Narhan (1984-89)*, BHU & D.K. Publishers, Delhi, 1994, pp. 29-35.
18. *IAR 1984-85*, pp. 162-3.
19. K.S. Saraswat, op. cit.
20. H.P. Ray in *An Encyclopaedia of Indian Archaeology* abbr. as *EIA*, ed. A. Ghosh, 2 vols, Munshiram Manoharlal, New Delhi, 1989, vol. I, pp. 5-6.
21. B.B. Lal in ibid., pp. 150-1.
22. R.N. Mehta in ibid., p. 187.
23. A. Ghosh in ibid., p. 127.
24. M.K. Dhavalikar in ibid., pp. 348-9.
25. M.D. Khare in ibid., pp. 348-9.
26. M.K. Dhavalikar in ibid., pp. 217-20.
27. H.P. Ray in ibid., pp. 265-7.
28. H.P. Ray in ibid., p. 188.
29. Ibid., pp. 312-13.
30. Ibid., pp. 315-16.
31. M.N. Deshpande in ibid., pp. 39-40.
32. M.K. Dhavalikar in ibid., pp. 416-17.

CHAPTER 4

Chalcolithic and Iron-NBPW Cultures Compared

The Two Cultural Deposits

More than a dozen chalcolithic complexes have been excavated in the mid-Ganga plains. Except for Chirand the dates of those which appear on the alluvial soil in the interior plains cannot be pushed much beyond 1000 BC.[1] The habitational deposits of the chalcolithic cultures of the mid-Ganga plains were poorer than those of western and central India where they ended around 1000-900 BC. At Champa near Bhagalpur the habitational deposits of the earliest settlers, who appear on the natural soil, measure about a metre. On the other hand, the Iron-NBPW habitational deposits measure 4.8 m.[2] Champa is situated on the alluvial soil, and significantly enough the Iron-NBPW deposits here is five times the pre-iron age deposits. At Sonpur the average thickness of the cultural deposit of the first phase of the chalcolithic period is about 61 cm.[3] Its second phase has an average cultural deposit of 3.05 m.[4] Therefore, the total cultural deposit of the chalcolithic period is 3.66 cm. The NBPW phase also seems to have been 3 m thick, as can be seen from SPRR XXXI: Section facing west.[5] At Taradih, in one of the mounds the deposit left by the neolithic people is 60 cm and that of the chalcolithic people is 1.5 m thick.[6] However, a separate mound shows the NBPW deposits to be roughly 2.5-3 m thick. In Rajgir the NBPW deposits are 2 m thick. But generally such deposits are much thicker in the sites found in the plains south of the Ganga in Bihar. For example, in Maner, 40 km west of Patna, in a small trench the chalcolithic deposits are 60 cm thick and the Iron-NPBW deposits are 3.75 m thick.[7] In Chirand, lying opposite Maner on the other side of the Ganga, the earliest habitation consisting of neolithic and chalcolithic complexes are 3.10 m thick while the NBPW deposits measure 1.84 m.[8] However, the 3 m deposit of pre-NBPW times consists of several sandy layers,[9] and consequently the pre-NBPW deposits are really not much thicker than the NBPW deposits.

In Vaishali the occupational deposits of the black-and-red layer representing the earliest settlement in one of the trenchs are 33 cm thick. On the other hand the NBPW deposits in all the areas measure on an average about 1.5 m.[10] A similar situation obtains at Khairadih in Ballia district. Here the earliest settlements characterised by the black-and-red ware (plain and painted), black slipped ware and red ware had a habitational deposit of 1.95 m; on the other hand the succeeding settlement marked by the NBPW and associated wares is 2.88 m thick.[11] The layers of the

NBPW phase reveal a higher quality of material culture. The real expansion of the settlements took place in *c.* 400-100 BC,[12] i.e. in the later phase of the NBPW. The settlement of Prahladpur resting on the high cliff on the right bank of the Ganga[13] near Varanasi has a pre- or proto-NBPW deposit of 1.04 m lying directly on the natural soil.[14] Iron appears in an upper deposit of the earliest phase,[15] and its illustrated specimen[16] appears to be a fragment of an arrowhead. In contrast the Iron-NBPW deposits measure 2.2 m in thickness.[17] Numerous iron objects appear as an important addition. The NBPW phase covers 500-163 BC.[18] The earliest settlements in Rajghat are attributed to 800 BC. Here pre-NBPW deposits comprising black slipped ware and black-and-red ware are 2.87 m thick at one place though the settlements are called 'sporadic'.[19] The total occupational deposit of the period to which both the NBPW and its preceding wares belong is nearly 5 m thick,[20] while the NBPW deposits account for nearly 2.13 m. The situation at Narhan on the Saryu in Gorakhpur district in the black-and-red ware phase, i.e. the earliest phase of settlement, is somewhat different. On Mound 1 black-and-red ware deposits measure 1 m[21], and the succeeding period marked by the frequency of black slipped ware has a deposit of 90 m.[22] The deposit of the NBPW phase which appears on Mound 2 is 75 cm thick though it shows more tools, cereals and structures than the deposit of the preceding phase.[23] The middle end of this period belongs to *c.* 260 BC.[24] At Ganwaria in Basti district the pre-NPBW deposits comprising black-and-red, black slipped and red wares measure 40 cm while the NBPW deposits are 1 m thick.[25] In Piprahwa in the same district the NBPW shards are found nominally. In Mahet in Bahraich district the black-and-red ware together with the NBPW deposit measure only 50 cm in thickness.[26]

At Shringaverapur located on the Ganga at a distance of

about 60 km north of Allahabad the earliest settlement marked by the use of red ware is about 30 to 60 cm thick. Though it is attributed to *c.* 1500-1000 BC,[27] its thin deposits make this dating doubtful. The succeeding settlement is distinguished by black-and-red and black slipped wares, and its deposit is 1.35 m thick.[28] The NBPW deposit is 2.1 m thick and is divided into three sub-periods.[29] Thus, generally occupational deposits in the settlements of Iron-NBPW phase are thicker than in the pre-NBPW phase. This is also true of Kausambi, Sravasti, Rajghat, Sohgaura and Narhan. However, the NBPW complexes in the plains of eastern U.P. and north Bihar, though older, are less thick in deposits than those in the plains south of the Ganga in Bihar. This may suggest more developed life in the southern plains. Why the NBPW deposits are less thick in Chirand, Vaishali, Khairadih, etc., needs to be explained.

Size and Number of NBPW Settlements

The NBPW age settlements increased considerably in size and number in the Ganga Yamuna Doab,[30] but this is more true of those in the mid-Ganga basin.[31] The habitational area of the Iron-NBPW phase is larger than that of the pre-Iron-NBPW phase. In the Maner mound the NBPW area spreads over 1 sq. km,[32] and in Chirand it measures 1 km x 125 m[33] and is nearly three times the neolithic-chalcolithic area. In Champa the NBPW area measures seven to eight times the chalcolithic area.[34] In Taradih its spread is more than ten times[35] the chalcolithic spread. In Vaishali the NBPW is spread over an area of 25 sq. km.[36]

Surface finds show nearly 450 NBPW sites in the mid-Ganga plains, though every site may not be as old as *c.* 500 BC. An exploration of Sultanpur district in eastern U.P. shows very few settlements in the pre-sixth century BC.[37]

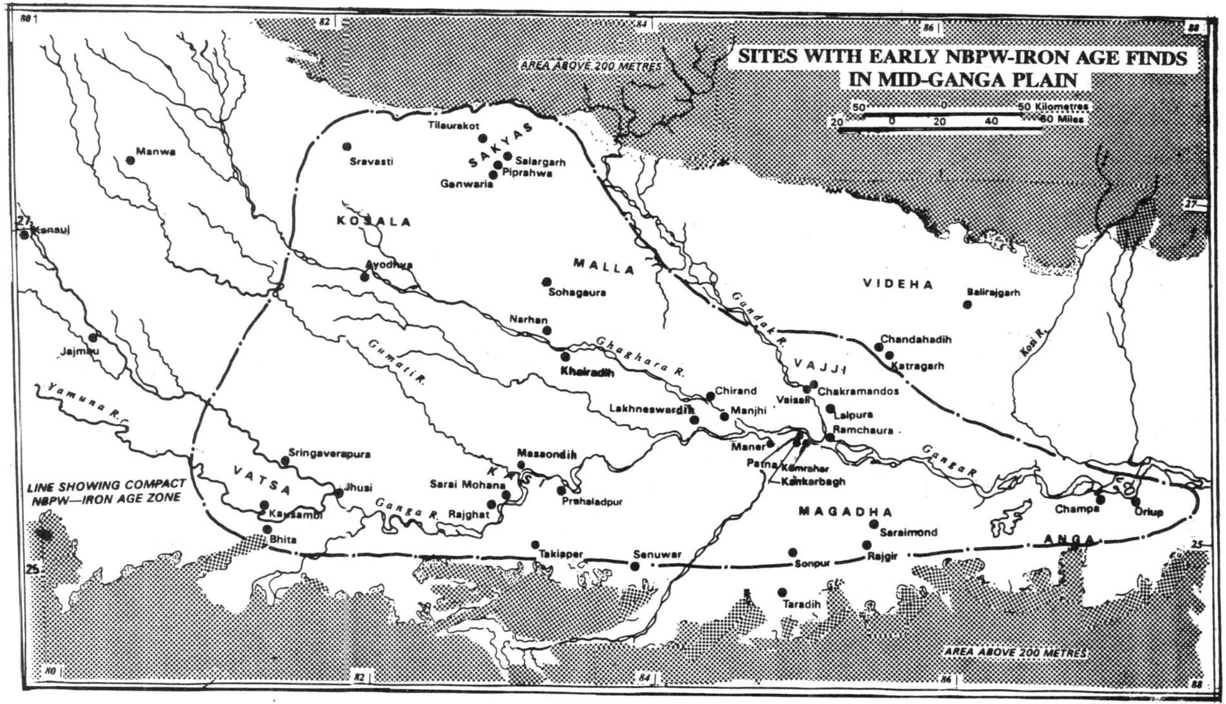

MAP 2: SITES WITH EARLY-NBPW-IRON AGE FINDS IN MID-GANGA PLAIN

This is also true of Basti district in the same region. Only after *c.* 600 BC did settlements burgeon in the mid-Ganga plains.

NOTES

1. Unfortunately the C^{14} dates for seven Taradih samples are not available so far. The radiocarbon dates for Khairadih read 1120±90 BC, 1030±160 BC and 940±150 BC; those for Narhan read 1100±110 BC, 1060±110 BC and 930+100 BC. Dates for Sohgaura are nearly two centuries eariler; 1335±113 BC and 1235±134 BC. P. Singh *et al.*, 'Explorations along the Kuwana River in Districts of Gorakhpur and Basti', *Prāgdhārā,* no. 1, 1990-1, U.P. State Archaeological Organisation, Lucknow, p. 76; *IAR 1988-89,* p. 110. The dates for the neolithic and chalcolithic phases in Chirand and Sohgaura appear in *Chronologies in Old World Archaeology*, ed. Robert W. Ehrich, vol. 1, *India,* by Gregory L. Possehl and Paul C. Rissman, The University of Chicago Press, Chicago, 1992, p. 463.
2. *IAR 1982-83,* p. 15
3. B.P. Sinha and B.S Verma, *Sonpur Excavations,* (*1956 and 1959-62*), Directorate of Archaeology and Museums, Bihar, Patna, 1977, p. 7.
4. Ibid., p. 8
5. B.P. Sinha and B.S Verma, op. cit., figure 3.
6. Communicated to me by A.K. Prasad.
7. *IAR 1985-86,* p. 11.
8. *IAR 1981-82,* pp. 13-14.
9. Information from A.K. Prasad.
10. Information from Sita Ram Roy, the excavator. Also see B.P. Sinha and S.R. Roy, *Vaiśālī Excavations, 1958-62,* Directorate of Archaeology and Museums, Bihar, Patna, 1969, plate XXI.
11. *IAR 1982-83,* p. 93.
12. *IAR 1985-86,* p. 78.
13. A. K. Narain and T.N. Roy, *The Excavations at Prahladpur, March-April 1963,* BHU University, 1968, p. 6.
14. Ibid., p. 65. However, on p. 9 of *Excavaation at Prahaladpur* the black-and-red ware deposit in layers 5 and 6 is given as 1.21 m.
15. Ibid.

16. Ibid., fig. 21, no. 4.
17. Ibid., p. 66.
18. Ibid.
19. A.K. Narain and T.N. Roy, *Excavations at Rajghat*, Part II, BHU, Varanasi, 1977, pp. 5-6.
20. Ibid., p. 7.
21. P. Singh and M. Lal, 'Narhan, 1983-85: A Preliminary Report of Archaeological Excavations', in *Bhāratī*, 1985, NS., no. 3, Varanasi, p. 120.
22. Ibid., pp. 120-1.
23. Ibid., pp. 121-2 supplemented by clarification communicated to me by P. Singh.
24. Ibid., p. 122.
25. Information from Lalchand Singh.
26. Information from D.K. Ambastha and S.K. Sinha for 1991-2 season.
27. *IAR 1978-79*, p. 57.
28. Ibid.
29. Ibid., p. 58.
30. Makkhan Lal, *Settlement History and Rise of Civilization in Ganga-Yamuna Doab from 1500 BC-300 AD*, B. R. Publishing House, Delhi, 1984, p. 255.
31. Ibid.
32. Information from B. Narayan.
33. Ibid.
34. Ibid.
35. Information from A.K. Prasad.
36. Information from Sita Ram Roy.
37. Ravindra Kumar, 'Archaeology of the Middle Gomati Basin with Special Reference to Sultanpur District, U.P.', Ph.D. Thesis, BHU, 1990.

CHAPTER 5

Migration of the Later Vedic People

Familiarity with the Eastern Region

The *Śatapatha Brāhmaṇa*, a text of the seventh century BC, clearly mentions the migration of the later Vedic people from the upper Gangetic to the mid-Ganga region. The *Atharva Veda* and the *Pañcaviṃśa Brāhmaṇa* (*c.* 1000-800 BC) show interregional familiarity. The first text refers to Magadha and Anga,[1] and both the texts mention the Vrātyas and Magadhas who lived in the east.[2] Even the *Ṛg Veda* speaks of a people called Kīkaṭas,[3] who are placed in the east. Thus, the Vedic people knew of the land lying in the east. Whether they knew its potentials is not clear though as iron users the later Vedic people may have been looking for the richer sources of iron lying in eastern Madhya Pradesh to the south of eastern U.P. plains, and more importantly in Singhbhum to the south of the Magadha plains. But they were certainly familiar with the mid-Ganga zone, and had the advantage of transport. They used the horse, and towards the end of the PGW phase they also used the spoked-wheel wagons.[4] Initially they may have used the Himalayan terai route where rivers were easy to cross and vegetation was not so thick; then the river route may have been adopted. Thus, armed with information and transport facilities small bands may have started eastward.

Literary Evidence Regarding Migration

The *Śatapatha Brāhmaṇa,* which mentions iron, speaks of the burning of the forest in north Bihar east of the Sadānīrā or the Gandak, which forms the boundary between Kosala and Videha. Before its crossing by Agni Vaiśvanara and Videgha Māthava the text describes the east as marshy, uncultivated, and uninhabited by the brahmanas. On the western bank of the river the land is described as being cultivated and inhabited by the brahmans.[5] The process of reclaiming the swampy land was known to the early settlers. At Rajghat in Varanasi the inhabitants cleared the swampy regions around *c.* 800 BC and settled as villagers practising agriculture.[6] It is possible that only some brahmanas and kṣatriyas, who formed the upper crust of society, came from the north and west. The brahmanas coming from the north (*odīcya*) were considered to be highly respectable. The lower order comprising the vaiśyas and sudras may have been mostly local people.

Spread of the Painted Grey Ware and the Black Slipped Ware

Later Vedic influence in the mid-Ganga plains evident from later Vedic texts is attested archaeologically. The later Vedic culture is identical with the PGW culture.[7] The spread of the grey ware and PGW indicates a tendency of the PGW people to migrate from north-west to south-east.[8] Vibha Tripathi notices a progressive lowering in the PGW dates from Noh, Atranjikhera and Hastinapur;[9] this suggests gradual migration from Haryana to western UP. PGW shards occur in Pariar. They appear in association with NBPW in Sravasti, Kausambi and Vaishali. Seven shards of PGW appear with the NBPW deposits of Vaishali.[10] Sometimes they are considered imitations, but they leave no doubt about contact between the upper Gangetic and mid-Ganga plains. At Sringaverapur some specimens of grey ware carry painted designs in which the painted surface shows the typical NBPW finish. All this suggests migration of the inhabitants of the upper Gangetic plains to the middle plains. Further, the NBPW from Mathura and Noh carry the calibrated radiocarbon dates of 600 BC and even of a century earlier. It seems that the NBPW people travelled from the west to eastern Uttar Pradesh and from there to the Bihar plains. It also appears that the NBPW is close to the PGW.

The affinity of the black slipped ware, which is prominent in eastern U.P. and Bihar,[11] with both the PGW and NBPW is significant. The ware appears with the PGW at Atranjikhera[12] and Hastinapur. The eastern black slipped ware is exactly similar in technique, texture and typology with the black slipped ware found in association with the PGW at Hastinapur.[13] Its painting tradition is akin to the PGW though the range of design is limited in comparison with the PGW.[14] In its polish the black slipped ware is nearer to the NBPW. It seems that the tradition associated with the PGW, the black slipped and the NBPW moved towards the east.[15] The NBPW flourished in the alluvial plains of eastern U.P. and Bihar, but the real breakthrough in the technology of pot-making appears in the black slipped ware[16] which precedes the NBPW at several sites including Narhan and Piprahwa in eastern U.P. and at Manjhi and Ramchaura (Hajipur) in Bihar.

Cremation Graves in the Mid-Ganga Basin

The presence of sacrificial altars and fire altars may be associated with the coming of the Vedic people, but such altars have not been found in eastern U.P. and in Bihar so far in the NBPW period. A terracotta sealing of the NBPW phase from Sonpur shows the depiction of *yupa* (sacrificial post).[17] Symbols of fire altar appear at Atranjikhera in the PGW phase,[18] but in the mid-Ganga plains fire altars appear in the third or the second century BC.[19] However post-cremation burials described in early Vedic texts are widely found. Several round pits at Sonpur in the chalcolithic layers[20] may be dated to *c.* 700 BC. 'Suspected' post-cremation pit burials in Chirand from the top level of the chalcolithic phase seem to be of the same date.[21] Since they are circular and similar to the Sonpur pits in their contents, we can be sure that they are burial pits.[22] According to Buddhist texts the corporeal relics of the Buddha were collected from the funeral pyre at Kusinagar or Kasia in Deoria district and divided among eight parties including the Licchavis of Vaishali, the Mallas of Kusinagar and the Śākyas of Kapilavastu. A mud stupa of the early NBPW period of Vaishali shows a small quantity of ashy earth deposited in a casket. It is attributed to the Licchavis and the remains in the casket are identified as those of the Buddha.[23] Kasia (Kusinagar) has a *nirvāna* stupa believed to have been erected over the site of Gautama Buddha's cremation, but its nucleus is not earlier than Aśoka.[24] The Dharmarājikā stupa at Sarnath attributed to Aśoka had a sandstone box with a marble relic casket, which contained a few pieces of bone, decayed pearls, gold leaves and some jewels.[25] A post-cremation burial of the third century BC in the form of the deposition of relics in the stupa appears in Piprahwa (considered identical with Kapilavastu) in Basti district.[26] Several hundred caskets containing pieces of bone, some of them half burnt, and other objects have been found here.[27] Special mention may be made of the relic caskets containing charred bones found in Piprahwa excavations. These are ascribed to the fifth-fourth centuries BC, i.e. the early phase of NBPW.[28] The chronology is broadly supported by the calibrated radiocarbon date for Piprahwa which has been dated to 391 BC.[29]

Contemporaneous with those of Piprahwa cremation graves in the form of stupa occur in Lauria-Nandangarh in Champaran district.[30] Rajgir shows as many as ten post-cremation burials in the early NBPW phase and their shapes are semioval or elliptical.[31] According to the *Śatapatha Brāhmaṇa* the Asuras (non-Vedic people) put up round tumuli over the remains of the dead body.[32] These instances suggest that by the sixth century BC cremation had come into vogue, and the practice of raising corporeal (*śārīrika*) stupa prevailed among the Buddhists. Undoubtedly cremation was introduced either directly by the Vedic people or under their strong influence. But the early post-cremation burial with round pits or urns, which are typical of the chalcolithic and megalithic people, may be an amalgam of the Vedic and the non-Vedic traditions. In any case cremation suggests the migration of the Vedic people.

Spread of the Horse and the Spoked Wheel

The wide use of horse is supported by the Vedic texts. Its importance in the mid-Ganga plains in the age of the Buddha can be inferred from many horse-based nomenclatures in the Pali texts.[33] We get many references to horses and chariots. The story of the horse named Kanthaka, which

Gautama Buddha mounted, when he decided to leave Kapilavastu is well known. So is the prominence of the wheel in Buddhist symbols. In the *Dighanikaya*, a text of *c.* 400 BC, the spoke is called *ara*,[34] which is also its modern form in Magadhi and Maithili. After 1000 BC, there is archaeological evidence to show that people were familiar with the horse in the upper and mid-Ganga plains. In the Indo-Gangetic divide horse bones are found at Bhagwanpura in Kurukshetra district[35] and are attributed to *c.* 1400-1000 BC. They also appear in Atranjikhera in Eta district in PGW and post-PGW phases.[36]

The NBPW levels of the upper and mid-Ganga plains show terracotta animal figurines including those of the horse and the elephant. The horse occurs in terracotta forms in the mid-level of the NBPW period at both Hastinapura[37] and Atranjikhera.[38] Some horse and elephant figures have riders attached to them.[39] From western U.P. the use of the domesticated horse may have spread to eastern U.P.

The remains of a horse attributed to the neolithic Mahagara, whose calibrated radiocarbon dates vary from 2569 to 1451 BC, are not considered to be those of the horse associated with the Aryans.[40] Bones of a large equine are found in Narhan in Gorakhpur district and assigned to 1000-800 BC though it is not clear whether they represent a true horse.[41] However, a terracotta figurine of a horse from this site has been dated to 600-200 BC.[42] The earliest clear evidence of the presence of the horse in the mid-Ganga basin occurs at Khairadih around 1000 BC.[43] The remains of certain wild and domesticated animals including the horse occur at Rajghat in the NBPW period (500-200 BC).[44] Terracotta figurines of the horse found in Prahladpur in Varanasi district are ascribed to *c.* 500 BC or the mid-phase of the excavated site.[45]

From 500 BC onwards the domesticated horse seems to have spread over a sizeable area of the mid-Ganga plains. The NBPW phase at Rajghat,[46] Prahladpur, Buxar,[47] Vaishali,[48] Chirand,[49] Sonpur,[50] Pataliputra,[51] and Champa[52] shows representations of the horse in terracotta. Two stone moulds showing figures of a horse have been found at Champa.[53] The horse was a favourite of the Pataliputra people.[54]

K.K. Sinha thinks that horse figurines are less numerous at U.P. sites between 300-50 BC but common between 50 BC-AD 300.[55] The horse symbolises speed, and therefore the one harnessed to the chariot is called *āśu* or quick, evidently connected with *aśva.*[56] Hence, this animal must have played an important part in the south-eastward advance of the Vedic colonisers, who probably came in small bands to the mid-Ganga plains from the Indo-Gangetic divide and upper Ganga plains.

Wheels, generally solid, were used in the Harappan carts and wagons.[57] Various types of wheel common in the Harappan period appear in the PGW levels of Ahicchatra in Bareilly district.[58] But in the alluvial plains of Bihar wheels are almost absent in the chalcolithic period in Taradih[59] and Sonpur and rare in the neolithic-chalcolithic phases in Chirand.[60] However, outside the mid-Ganga plains horse-drawn chariots were in use in the megalithic culture from the sixth century BC onwards.[61] The use of cart wheels can be inferred from terracotta objects found in Sonpur,[62] Pataliputra[63] and Vaishali.[64] The general use of carts is evidenced by terracotta toycarts and its fragments found in Chirand,[65] Sonpur,[66] Taradih[67] and elsewhere. Wheels also appear as symbols on punch-marked coins and uninscribed cast copper coins.[68]

Toy-cart wheels found at the mid-Ganga sites in the NBPW period suggest the use of both solid and spoked

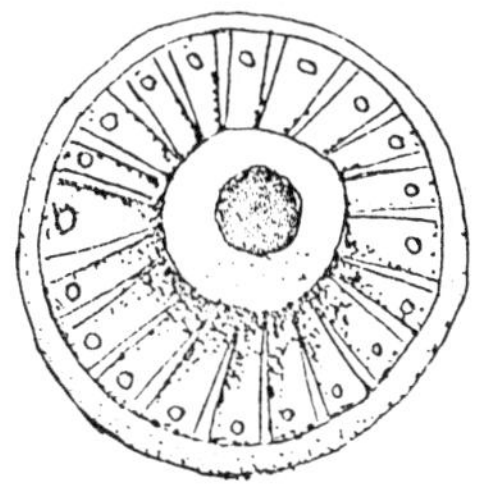

FIGURE 2 : MID-NBPW TERRACOTTA SPOKED WHEEL FROM CHAMPA

wheels. Solid wheels made of clay occur in the early layers of the NBPW period and those with spokes in its last phase at Atranjikhera[69] and Jakhera.[70] A wheel with an indication of spokes is found in the NBPW period of Sonpur.[71] Terracotta toy-cart wheels with impressed spokes and nails occur in both the early and middle levels of the NBPW phase in Vaishali.[72]

The widespread use of wheels and carts/wagons in the iron-using cultures of the mid-Ganga plains is in contrast with their near absence in the chalcolithic cultures of this area. The NBPW phase also gives several examples of spoked wheels. Their appearance meant lighter carts and faster speed. Thus, in the NBPW period in the mid-Ganga plains pedestrian or pack animal transport was reinforced by cart transport, which became faster because of the use of spokes. From the fourth-third century BC onwards toy-cart models became common in early historical sites including Kausambi, Bhita, Sonpur, etc. Significantly the spread of the use of the horse and the spoked wheel in the mid-Ganga plains was accompanied by the diffusion of the animal sacrifice, cremation and above all by the spread of the Indo-Aryan language which assumed a written shape as can be seen from the Aśokan edicts issued from Pataliputra. All these traits, resulting from the spread of the Vedic culture must have influenced the existing social and political organisation of the mid-Ganga plains.

NOTES

1. A.A. Macdonell and A.B. Keith, *Vedic Index of Names and Subjects,* II, Motilal Banarsidass, rpt, 1967, pp. 116-18.
2. Ibid., pp. 342-5.
3. Ibid., I, p. 159.
4. Supra, pp. 46-7.
5. *Śatapatha Brāhmaṇa,* 1.4.1.14-17. The Sadānīrā is sometimes also identified with the Rāptī or Acirāvātī on the southern bank of which the Sarasvastī was situated.
6. A.K. Narain and T.N. Roy, *Excavation at Rajghat,* pt. II, BHU, Varanasi, 1977, pp. 5-6.
7. This view appears in R.S. Sharma, *Material Culture and Social Formations in Ancient India,* 1983, ch. IV , and finds favour with A. Ghosh in *EIA,* 1 (1989), p. 75, and with B.B. Lal in A.H. Dani and V.M. Masson, eds., *A History of Civilizations of Central Aisa,* UNESCO Publishing, Paris, 1992, vol. I, 439 with fn. 36.
8. R.S. Sharma, *Material Culture and Social Formations in Ancient India,* pp. 172-3.
9. 'A Macro-Level Study of Painted Grey Ware Culture', *Prāgdhārā,* no. 1, 1990-1, p. 93.
10. B.P. Sinha and S.R. Roy, *Vaiśālī Excavations, 1958-62,* pp. 40-1, 43.
11. A.K. Misra, 'Ganga Valley: Twilights on its Problems as revealed in Archaeological Excavations', in *Prāgdhārā,* no. 1, 1990-1, p. 107.
12. R.C. Gaur, *Excavations at Atranjikhera,* Delhi, 1983, p. 124. In Period III, called the PGW culture, the black slipped ware

shards greatly outnumber the PGW shards, ibid.

13. T.N. Roy, *The Ganges Civilization*, Ramanand Vidya Bhawan, New Delhi, 1983, p. v.
14. A.K. Misra, op. cit., p. 107.
15. A.K. Misra thinks that the black slipped ware travelled from the east to the west (ibid).
16. This is the view of several archaeologists including R.C. Gaur and K.M. Srivastava.
17. B.P. Sinha and B.S. Verma, *Sonpur Excavations*, p. 100, plate 24, no. 14.
18. The date attributed to PGW is 1200-600 BC (*EIA*, II, pp. 26-7), which may be brought down by 200 years or more.
19. D.R. Patil, *The Antiquarian Remains in Bihar*, K.P. Jayaswal Research Institute, Patna 1963, p. 27.
20. B.P. Sinha and B.S. Verma, *Sonpur Excavations*, p. 8.
21. *IAR 1968-69*, p. 5; cf. *EIA*, I, p. 98.
22. This view has been communicated to me by S.R. Roy who visited the site at the time of excavation.
23. B.P. Sinha and S.R. Roy, *Vaiśālī Excavations, 1958-62*, pp. 16-22.
24. *EIA*, II, p. 247.
25. *EIA*, I, p. 270; II, pp. 397-8.
26. But the identification is disputed, *EIA*, II, p. 345; *Annual Report ASI, 1906-7*, pp. 119ff; *1935-36*, pp. 55ff.
27. *EIA*, I, p. 271.
28. K.M. Srivastava, *Dicovery of Kapilavastu*, Books & Books, New Delhi, 1986, p. 47.
29. Gregory, L. Possehl, ed., 'Radiocarbon Dates for South Asian Archaeology', University of Pennsylvania, Philadelphia, June 1989 (unpublished), p. 26, Calib-2.
30. Ibid., II, p. 365; W.C. Peppe and V.A. Smith, 'The Piprahwa Stupa contianing Relics of Buddha', *JASB*, 1898, p. 573ff.
31. *Ancient India*, no. 7, pp. 69-70.
32. XIII. 8.1.5.
33. G.P. Malalasekera, *Dictionary of Pāli Proper Names*, vol. I, rpt, The Pali Text Society, London, 1974, pp. 220-9; s.v. *assa*, T.W. Rhys Davids and W. Stede, *Pali-English Dictionary*, PTS, London, 1921.
34. s.v. *ara*, *Pali-English Dictionary*, op. cit.
35. Jagat Pati Joshi, *Excavation at Bhagwanpura 1975-76, and Other Explorations & Excavations 1975-81 in Haryana, Jammu*

and Kashmir and Punjab, Archaeological Survey of India, New Delhi, 1993, pp. 143-7.
36. R.C. Gaur, *Excavation at Atranjikhera,* Motilal Banarsidass, Delhi, 1983, p. 462.
37. *Ancient India,* nos. 10-11 (1954-1955), p. 86, plate 42, fig. 3.
38. R.C. Gaur, *Excavations at Atranjikhera,* 1983, pp. 366-9.
39. *EIA,* I, p. 339.
40. G.R. Sharma, V.D. Mishra, D. Mandal, B.B. Mishra and J.N. Pal, *Beginnings of Agriculture,* Abinash Prakashan, Allahabad, 1980, pp. 220-1 with fn. on p. 221; Possehl, 'Radiocarbon Dates for South Asian Archaeology' (unpublished), p. 13, Calib-2.
41. U.C. Chattopadhyaya, 'Report on Faunal Remains in Narhan' in Purushottam Singh, *Exacavations at Narhan (1984-89)*, BHU & D.K. Publishers, Delhi, 1994, pp. 251-2; cf. *IAR 1984-85,* p. 90; *IAR 1985-86,* p. 123. Purushottam Singh and Makkhan Lal, 'Narhan: 1983-85: A Preliminary Report of Archaeological Excavations', *Bhāratī,* NS, no. 3, pp. 120-1.
42. P. Singh, *Excavations at Narhan,* pp. 34, 153.
43. Information from B.P. Singh on the basis of Register of Antiquities.
44. A.K. Narain and T.N. Roy, *Excavations at Rajghat,* pt. II, pp. 8-9.
45. A.K. Narian and T.N. Roy, *The Excavations at Prahladpur, March-April 1963,* Varanasi, 1968, pp. 13, 45-6.
46. A.K. Narian and T.N. Roy, *Excavations at Rajghat,* pt. II, pp. 8-9.
47. *EIA,* II, p. 89.
48. Krishna Dev and Vijayakant Mishra, *Vaishali Excavation: 1950,* Vaishali Sangh, Vaishali, 1961, p. 56; B.P. Sinha and S.R. Roy, *Vaiśālī Excavations,* p. 160.
49. Information from B.S. Verma.
50. B.P. Sinha and B.S. Verma, *Sonpur Excavations,* Patna, 1977, p. 119, p. 100
51. B.P. Sinha and L.A. Narain, *Pataliputra Excavations,* pp. 43-4.
52. *IAR 1971-72,* p. 5 and pl. XI B.
53. Ibid.
54. B.P. Sinha and L.A. Narain, *Pataliputra Excavations 1955-56,* Patna, 1970, p. 10.
55. *EIA,* I, p. 136.
56. *Śatapatha Brāhmaṇa,* V. 3.3.3.
57. *EIA,* I, p. 337.
58. Ibid.

59. Information from A.K. Prasad.
60. Information from B.S. Verma.
61. *EIA*, I, p. 336.
62. B.P. Sinha and B.S. Verma, *Sonpur Excavations*, pp. 123-5.
63. B.P. Sinha and L.A. Narain, *Pataliputra Excavations 1955-56*, Patna, 1970, p. 47.
64. B.P. Sinha and S.R. Roy, *Vaiśālī Excavations*, pp. 202-3.
65. Information from B.S. Verma.
66. B.P. Sinha and B.S. Verma, *Sonpur Exavations*, pp. 124-5.
67. *IAR 1985-86*, p. 8.
68. B.P. Sinha and B.S. Verma, *Sonpur Excavations*, p. 95.
69. R.C. Gaur, op. cit., p. 374.
70. Information from M.D.N. Sahi.
71. B.P. Sinha and B.S. Verma, *Sonpur Excavations*, p. 124, plate XXXIX, no.7.
72. B.P. Sinha and S.R. Roy, *Vaiśālī Excavations 1958-62*, pp. 202-3.

CHAPTER 6

Cultural Fusion and Social Transformation

Ethnic and Cultural Fusion

The later Vedic culture identical with the PGW culture led to the rise of civilization in the upper Ganga plains and also contributed to this process in the mid-Ganga basin. The later Vedic phase shows the beginnings of both social differentiation and state apparatus. Knowledge of these institutions may have travelled to the east. The 'interaction of two cultural and ethnic traditions' is called 'a historical accident'.[1] But, as shown earlier,[2] the mixing of the PGW-Vedic and the pre-NBPW non-Vedic streams in the mid-Ganga plains was to be expected. Many PGW sites in the upper Gangetic plains were single-culture sites which did not last beyond a century. Probably the settlers were forced to move eastward in search of subsistence when the local soil became unproductive. As the Vedic people advanced further east they encountered the chalcolithic culture of the mid-Ganga plains. Both cultures were familiar with iron and cereals. But though iron appears at most excavated PGW sites, only a limited number of black-and-red ware sites of the late chalcolithic phase shows iron. Iron objects from both cultures show little carburisation, and mainly represent weaponry. Both the upper and mid-Ganga peoples produced more or less the same cereals. The PGW or the later Vedic people used wooden shares in the upper Ganga plains, but we have no clue about the shares of the middle plains. However, the PGW, or later Vedic people, enjoyed some advantages. They were spread over a compact area and were superior in war and transportation because of the use of the horse and also of the spoked wheel. Though they practised animal sacrifice, they domesticated cattle for milk. They were well on their way to the formation of a complex society and a territorial state. They seem to have been literate, and used the widely-spoken Indo-Aryan language and rich literature laden with rituals. In contrast the mid-Ganga people were basically hunters, herdsmen and hoe agriculturists. Their artefacts indicate that mere familiarity with iron and cereals did not take them too far. Their ability to produce goods in quality or quantity did not improve much, and they continued to live in small scattered settlements. This again reminds us of the use of the horse, which though known in the sixth millennium BC, became really important after 3000 BC.

The Vrātya Factor

Sufficient remains of neolithic-chalcolithic times have not been discovered making it difficult to understand the nature of the society of that age. Lack of pre-500 BC burials, and almost total absence of structures, ritual centres and objects of body decoration make it difficult to visualize any sharp social or kin-based differentiation. Ethnological data are also insufficient. The descriptions of the Kīkaṭas in the *Ṛg Veda* and those of the Vrātyas in the later Vedic texts cannot be easily related to the culture of the neolithic-chalcolithic people living in the mid-Ganga plains. The name of the Kīkaṭa king Pramaganda, seems 'un-Āryan',[3] and they are assigned to Haryana or to Magadha on the ground that they are non-Vedic people. They are condemned as people who do not deserve to keep cows because they do not perform sacrifice which require the use of milk.[4] A Gond clan believes that milk is meant for young animals and meat for human beings. Thus, the Kīkaṭas may have been a beef-eating pastoral people, ignorant of the virtues of dairy farming. They may have been a segmentary, egalitarian group.

Reference to the Vrātyas in the *Atharva Veda* and *Pañcaviṃśa Brāhmaṇa* also called *Tāṇḍya Mahābrāhmaṇa* do not provide a clear picture. The mystical story of the dispersals of the Vrātyas in all four directions given in Book XV of the *Atharva Veda* makes it difficult to confine them exclusively to the east. However, in all the dispersals a *māgadha*, literally a resident of Magadha but with its secondary meaning of bard, appears as a constant companion of the Vrātya chief, which suggests that the latter was closely associated with Magadha around 800 BC or so when Book XV was composed. A post-Vedic text, the *Lāṭyāyana Śrautasūtra,* states that during the performance of the Vrātyastomas for the initiation of the Vrātya into the fold of brahmanism sacrificial gifts are made to a second class or inferior brahmana (*brahmabandhu*) belonging to the land of Magadha (*magadhadeśīya*).[5] This supplementary reference attests the connection of the Vrātyas with Magadha.

The appearance of the Vrātyas in Magadha is a case of migration. The term 'Vrātya' is a Vedic word derived from the term '*vrāta*', which means a kin-based group or multitude. The Vrātyas were therefore an early Vedic group who spoke an Indo-Aryan language.[6] It is said that they neither study the Vedas nor do they plough or trade,[7] which shows them to be basically a pastoral people.

Metaphorically they are identified with the Maruts, for Dyutāna, who belonged to the Maruts, was their householder.[8] The *Pañcaviṃśa Brāhmaṇa* divides the Vrātyas into condemned (*nindita*), 'eldest' (*jyeṣṭha*) and 'youngest' (*kaniṣṭha*), and accordingly prescribes different rites for their ordination.[9] It is difficult to comment on the 'condemned'. But according to one view the eldest were brought into the Vrātya way of life earlier and the youngest later.[10] In our view the 'eldest' may have been the earliest to arrive and the 'youngest' may have been the late comers. As such the 'eldest' or seniors may have enjoyed certain advantages. It is significant that consequent upon initiation the younger were allowed to keep cattle which led to their prosperity.[11] The description of the Vrātya *gṛhapati* (literally, the head of the household) with a turban, a whip, a bow, black garment and two skins, a rough wagon (*vipatha*), two round ornaments and a *niṣka* or silver ornament,[12] suggests that he was a warrior chief. He rode a car, probably driven by oxen. He also occupied a seat called *āsandī*, which is also mentioned in the *rajasūya* sacrifice.[13] His retinue consisted of a harlot, a minstrel (*māgadha*), a charioteer and two attendants. The dress and equipment of the Vrātya chief remind us of wheeled wagons, arrowheads and semiprecious stones, which are found in both the upper Ganga and mid-

Ganga plains in pre-500 BC times. Wheeled wagons are, however, absent in the chalcolithic Magadha, and were probably introduced by the Vrātya chiefs. The other Vrātyas have upper garments with red border and corded fringes, with strings on each side; each of them has a pair of shoes and doubly-joined goats' hides.[14]

These seem to be the followers or kinsmen of the *gṛhapati*. The fact that they had a pair of shoes (*upānaha*) each shows them to be well off. It is significant that the term *panahī* derived from *upanaha* is still current in some Indo-Aryan dialects of Bihar. However, the two types of dress and equipment suggest a clear distinction between the chief and his followers. We may note that each one of his followers presented thirty-three cows to the chief.[15] This indicates that in a pastoral set-up the chief was entitled to receive such a presentation. The Sūtras speak of warriors (*yaudhas*) and saints (*arhants*) among the Vrātyas.[16] Therefore, the Vrātyas are divided into three higher social orders including the householders (*gṛhapati*).[17] But this division may apply to post-Vedic times to which the Sūtras belong. The earliest Vrātyas correspond to sudras, for they do not read the Veda. The term *arhant* is used for a Buddhist monk, which suggests that by the fourth century BC Buddhism influenced the Vrātyas in eastern India.

Apparently the existing tribal people of the mid-Ganga plains did not have much of social differentiation. Men may have been engaged in big game hunting and in fighting, and women in agriculture. However, women and children may have taken part in small game hunting. Large hearths from Taradih[18] suggest communal kitchen and eating at one place. Probably the chiefs distinguished themselves from their ordinary kinsmen by the use of semiprecious stones to symbolize their higher higher status. They may also have used skin-rubbers. More importantly they may have enjoyed easy access to copper and to weapons used in war and hunting. All this may have added to the authority of the chief. Even then the mid-Ganga people seem to have been more egalitarian than the PGW/Vedic people.

It is likely that the Vrātyas migrated eastwards and in other directions on account of the hostility of the more brahmanised sections of the Vedic community. The later Vedic texts refer to natural calamities which forced the brahmanas to leave the Kuru-Pañcāla land and migrate towards the east.[19] The fact that the eastern customs were disliked by the Vedic people[20] did not deter them from moving eastward. The *Atharva Veda* is familiar with the Magadhas and Angas to whom the *takman* fever is supposed to have been despatched. Therefore, the Vrātyas seem to have moved to the east earlier than the group of the brahmana and the kṣatriya mentioned in the *Śatapatha Brāhmaṇa*. Further, the Vrātya were a non-brahmanised people unlike the *Śatapatha* migrants. The Kosalas and the Kāśīs are called the offspring of the *Śatapatha* hero Videgha Māthava who migrated to Videha along with his priest Gotama Rāhugaṇa and other brahmanas, all led by the Fire God Agni Vaiśvānara.

The Vrātya band and the Videgha Māthava group may be identified with the users of the PGW, black slipped ware and even with the earliest NBPW people from the Kuru-Pañcāla land or western U.P. and its neighbourhood. The cattle-rearing Vrātyas may have merged with the mid-Ganga pastoralists, but the Videgha Māthava group seem to have introduced the brahmana and kṣatriya orders. The two performed the *aśvamedha* sacrifice in order to strengthen the powers of the chieftains leading to the concentration of authority in the hands of a class of warriors. The *Śāṅkhāyana Śrautasūtra* describes Jala Jātūkarṇya as the *purohita* or priest of the kings of Kosala, Kāśī and Videha,[21] and the oldest

Buddhist text, the *Suttanipāta,* speaks of animal sacrifices in Kosala in the days of the Buddha.

The institutional ideas and practices brought in by the people from the Kuru-Pañcāla land probably changed the social and political configuration of the mid-Ganga plains. The Vrātya chieftainship may have fused with the local chieftainship, and its symbols of authority such as turban, chariot, charioteer, jewels and semiprecious stones may have served as new or additional signs of authority and differentiation in the mid-Ganga plains. The authority of the chieftain class may have been enhanced by the advent of the kṣatriyas/rājanyas who were both warriors and also pioneer settlers and farmers.

Privileges for Pioneers

The earliest settlers in a virgin area may have received respect and obedience from those who came later. The appearance of the elements of material culture such as PGW, the horse, the spoked wheel, cremation, etc., at intervals suggests the continuous migration of bands of people from the west to the plains of eastern U.P. and Bihar. Among the Oraons in the south Bihar plateau the descendants of the families which were the first to settle in a village enjoy special regard.[22] It is thought that in the hazy period of migrations and village foundations they held priestly office or chieftainship.[23] Families not sprung from the parties who first cleared the jungle and broke up the soil are accounted common citizens.[24] A small percentage of Oraon tenants claim to be *addiyar* or the descendants of the original settlers, who cleared the primeval jungles and first cultivated the fields. These descendants enjoy such fields as are 'practically rent-free'.[25]

The tradition of rewarding founders of settlements who

brought virgin land under cultivation continued in later times. In the *Arthaśāstra* Kauṭilya enjoins the king to allow concessions and exemptions to the first settlers of the *janapada* or the village,[26] but recommends neither permanent exemption to the first farmers not to their descendants. Similarly, among the Oraons *nāl* lands newly created by a raiyat's own industry out of his own high ground portion, state waste or jungle tract are semi-privileged in the sense that they go rent-free for the first three annual crops.[27]

Once such privileged properties were created it became necessary to develop a strong, premanent leadership or authority to protect them. Whether a chief or a warrior obtained certain economic rewards by dint of his bravery in war or by his skill in farming and founding settlements, he perpetuated these rewards foi his progeny through force, custom, precedent, rituals and genealogical ideology. The recepients formed a close kin group which wanted to regularise and legitimatise their privileges at the cost of the other kin groups related to them.

The story of Videgha Māthava and Agni Vaiśvānara suggests the pioneering role of the kṣatriya and brahmana settlers in the east of the Gandak. They did not have to pay taxes probably because of this role coupled with the military and religious services that they rendered to the community. The non-payment of taxes was continued by their descendants, a fact documented by both Richard Fick and P.V. Kane. Thus, social, enomomic and political distinctions may have emerged among those Vedic people who migrated from the land of the Kuru-Pañcālas or western U.P. and the adjacent areas. These people were already familiar with the presence of the proto-state and social differentiation. The leading families may have also used rituals found in the Śrautasūtras and Gṛhyasūtras to strengthen their hold.

Social Stratification

The cremation burials of about 500 BC-300 BC indicate social differentiation. The Vaishali funeral casket buried in a mud mound belongs to the pre-brick stage of about the fifth-fourth centuries BC. Similarly, the Piprahwa caskets discovered in excavation by K.M. Srivastava belong to fifth-fourth centuries BC. What is remarkable, the Vaishali casket contains ashes together with a piece of gold, a punch-marked copper coin, two glass beads and one shell conch.[28] Some burials attributed to *c.* 300 BC in Piprahwa and Lauriya Nandangarh also contain punch-marked coins and gold leaves along with ashes and charred bones. Their contents clearly suggest social differentiation in the mid-Ganga plains in the fifth century BC and later.

Cultural exchanges and social accommodation may have brought together the privileged interest groups from the two cultural streams. The emergent group may have formed the state and laid down rules for the regulation of a hierarchical society. While the Vedic people acquired land and pastures together with important cereals, the non-Vedic people learnt the use of the horse, the spoked wheel and dairy-based domestication; they may also have been made literate. Their coming together may have promoted iron technology. Perhaps the later Vedic people introduced paddy transplantation which boosted production.

The interplay between the two ethnic and cultural groups gave rise to Middle Indo-Aryan languages known as Pali and Prakrit. The vocabulary for plants, animals, tools, crafts, etc., found in these languages suggests either the superimposition of the Indo-Aryan subsistence terms over the existing ones or the borrowing of these terms from the Vedic people because of the introduction of some new modes of subsistence by them. Along with Sanskrit these languages facilitated communication and created a favourable climate for the formation of the state and stratified society.

NOTES

1. George Erdosy, *Urbanisation in Early Historic India, BAR* International Series, 430, Oxford, 1988, p. 130.
2. See ch. 5.
3. *VI*, II, p. 38
4. *Ṛg Veda*, III.53.14. Medieval authorities place the Kīkaṭas in Magadha.
5. A.C. Banerjea, *Studies in the Brāhmaṇas*, Motilal Banarsidass, Delhi, 1963, pp. 169-70.
6. *PB*, XVII.1.9.
7. *na hi brahmacaryaṃ caranti na kṛṣim na vāṇijyam*, ibid., XVII.1.2.
8. Ibid., XVII.1.7.
9. XVII.2-4 sections.
10. A.C. Banerjea, op. cit., pp. 161-3.
11. *PB*, XVII, 2.4.
12. *AV*, XV. 2.1; *PB*, XVII.1.14; cf. A.C. Banerjea, op. cit., p. 126. The *vipatha* is described as a wagon of the easterners (*prācya-ratha*) in *Lāṭyāyana Śrautasūtra* (VI, II, p. 46).
13. A.C. Banerjea, op. cit., p. 126.
14. *PB*, XVII.1.16.
15. *PB*, XVII.1.17.
16. *VI*, II, p. 343.
17. Erdosy in F.R. Allchin with contributions from others, *The Archaeology of Early Historic South Asia*, CUP, 1995, p. 91.
18. *IAR 1984-85*, p. 10, *IAR* 1985-86, p. 8.
19. H.C. Raychaudhuri, *Political History of Ancient India*, 7th edn, University of Calcutta, 1972, p. 41 with fn. 5.
20. *VI*, II, p. 46.
21. *VI*, II, pp. 298, 409.
22. A. Grignard, S.J. *Hahn's Oraon Folk-lore in the Original: A critical text translation and notes*, Government Printing, Bihar and Orissa, Gulzarbagh, Patna, 1931, p. 2.
23. Ibid.
24. Ibid., p. 3.
25. Ibid., p. 2.
26. *AŚ*, II.1.
27. A. Grignard, S.J., op. cit., p. 16.
28. B.P. Sinha and S.R. Roy, *Vaiśālī Excavations. 1958-62*, p. 22.

CHAPTER 7

The Role of Iron[1]

Historical Stages

Iron appears in the mid-Ganga plains in the late chalcolithic phase around 800 BC or a little earlier. In the lower Gangetic zone, in Pandurajardhibi, it is attributed to 1200-600 BC,[2] but the chalcolithic layers of Champa and Oriup in Bhagalpur and Jhimjhimia[3] near Rajmahal, despite the relative proximity of these sites to the West Bengal site, do not reveal signs of iron. The extremely limited use of iron did not significantly affect the life of the people. Two stages appear in its use.[4] The first stage is marked by the use of low grade ores, absence of carburisation and manufacture of weapons. It generally shows wrought iron. A single radiocarbon date from the chalcolithic phase in Hatigra in West Bengal has led to the dating of the advent of low carbon steel around 1000 BC.[5] However, five dates assigned to 'Early Iron Age' layers from the same site range between AD 385 and AD 990,[6] and dates for low carbon steel from other places are not earlier than the sixth century BC.

After a gestation of about 500 years there began the second stage in the history of iron in northern India. This reminds us of the history of the use of the horse. Though the animal first appeared in the sixth millennium BC, it came into wider use only after 3000 BC. The second stage in the history of iron is marked by carburisation resulting in mild or semi-steel, by the use of high grade ores and, more importantly, by the manufacture of tools meant for production. Although Singhbhum in the south Bihar plateau contains the richest and high grade iron ores, evidence for the use of these ores in the mid-Ganga plains is not earlier than *c.* 600 BC.[7] These ores containing more of pure iron and less of impurities came to be smelted during the NBPW phase. Earlier low grade ores, which can be easily smelted, were used.[8] Therefore, earliest iron artefects were neither numerous nor effective. Around the third century BC the practice of quenching and tampering iron artefacts and thus hardening them appeared in Pandurajardhibi and Khairadih. This process is attested by the *Suttanipāta*, a pre-Mauryan Buddhist text.[9] Iron objects of the second half of the first millennium BC from eastern India are held technologically superior to those from western U.P. or Gujarat,[10] but the view needs further supportive evidence.

It is important to stress the functional distinction between the two stages in the history of the use of iron. In the first stage iron tools were mainly used for war and hunting. However, in the second stage from *c.* 600 BC onwards though they continued to be used by hunters and warriors they were mainly used by farmers and artisans.

Iron artefacts from the chalcolithic phase in the mid-Ganga basin are far outnumbered by those recovered from the NBPW layers. Though the Rajghat excavations show only one or two iron objects in the pre-NBPW layers, 100 slags and artefacts including axes, chisels, sickles, etc., showing 'unprecedented growth of crafts and industries' are found at the same site.[11] This is also true of Chirand, Sonpur and Taradih. Chisels and nails from the black-and-red ware phases at Taradih[12] and Narhan[13] may not be earlier than *c.* 600 BC.

Despite the corrosive character of the soil, iron objects appear at about three dozen excavated sites in mid-Ganga plains. Though arrowheads and spearheads continue to be used in the NBPW phase, axes, chisels, sickles, shares, knives, nails, etc., appear in good numbers. Champa shows a good many iron objects.[14] The flourishing iron industry at Sonpur in the NBPW phase is attested by the discovery of two crucibles and many knives, blades, lances, spearheads, arrowheads, axes, chisels, nails, door-fittings and rings which were used in crafts, construction work and agriculture. Fifty-five pieces of iron objects appear in this place, and some of these such as an arrowhead and a lance are socketed.[15] These iron objects are extremely corroded.[16] Similar is the condition of Pataliputra iron objects, which belong to NBPW and other periods, and include daggers, nails, pans, axes and sickles.[17]

Iron and Agriculture

While iron axes were used in cutting trees, iron hoe and share were used in breaking the hard clayey soil of the plains of Magadha as well as of the plains lying north of the Ganga in Bihar and eastern U.P. The new alluvium found in the mid-Ganga plains could not be broken by wooden

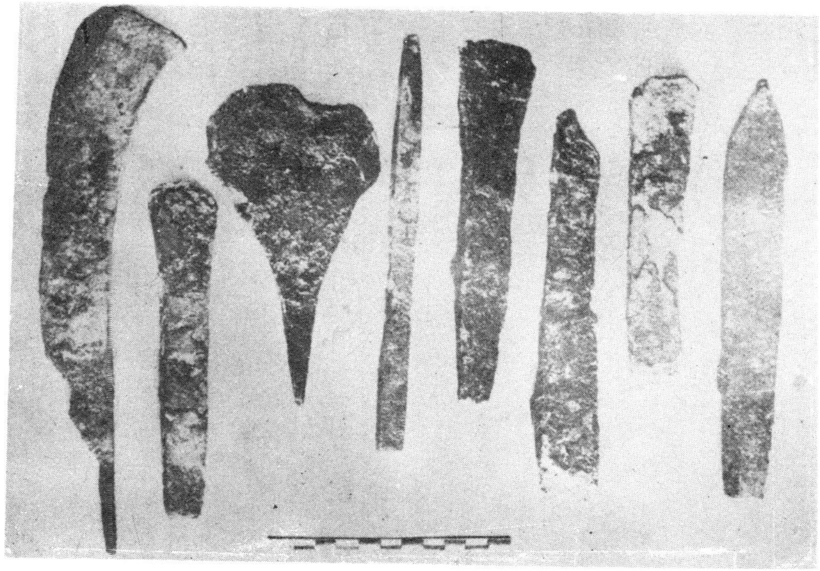

PLATE 2: EARLY AND MID-NBPW IRON PLOUGHSHARES AND OTHER IRON AGRICULTURAL TOOLS FROM PIPRAHWA-GANWARIA

ploughshares except in the sandy and loamy areas. Iron shares of about 600 BC occur in Ganwaria. An iron share from the upper levels of Period I (pre-NBPW) is called 'an outstanding find'.[18] Several iron shares, sickles, edges (*khurpas*), knives, etc., all meant for agricultural and household purposes dominated the finds in Period II (NBPW).[19] Iron shares also appear at four or five other places and belong to *c.* 500 BC.[20] Similarly, several iron axes and sickles occur in the NBPW phase in Sonpur.[21] The deluxe nature of NBPW suggests that it was mainly used by the higher strata of the urban people, but several sickles occur in NBPW sites, and they may have been used mainly for agrarian purposes.

From *c.* 1500 BC onwards the main cereals were known in several parts of the mid-Ganga basin. They continued in the Iron-NBPW phase. In this age the tools and methods of agriculture underwent a radical change. The use of iron hoes, shares and sickles boosted production, which was also helped by irrigation. Between 700-200 BC rice, barley, wheat, green gram or *mung*, gram, chick-pea, pea and *khesārī* can be found in Khairadih.[22] Several important additions are made to the list in the age of the Buddha. Mustard is mentioned in the early Pali texts. Both mustard and sesame oil may have been used in cooking. Further, a great variety of pulses began to be cultivated. Finally, sugar cane, which requires deep ploughing, is mentioned in the Pali and Sanskrit texts.

More importantly, paddy transplantation seems to have appeared in the NBPW phase. The mention of the *plāśuka* variety of *vrīhi* or paddy in the *Śatapatha Brāhmaṇa*[23] (seventh century BC) is a reference to a transplanted variety which ripens quickly. But transplantation is clearly indicated by Pali and Prakrit texts. Wet rice cultivation revolutionized agriculture by increasing paddy production nearly two and a half times. It is also significant that in the alluvial plains of the mid-Ganga and outside this zone rice yield in the pre-

PLATE 3: EARLY AND MID-NBPW IRON AGRICULTURAL AND OTHER TOOLS FROM PIPRAHWA-GANWARIA

industrial phase of technology was much larger than that of wheat. Thus, in terms of high productivity rice producing areas had a distinct edge over other areas.

Coupled with the use of iron tools in agriculture, paddy transplantation made available considerable surplus with which the state apparatus and complex society comprising priests, rulers, soldiers, merchants, artisans, professionals, etc., could be maintained.[24] Equally significant was the rise of the cites around 500 BC and their growth in subsequent times. Rearing of cattle and other animals was inherited by the chalcolithic people from their predecessors. However, the pre-NBPW people reared cattle mainly for meat which formed the principal item in their food.[25] Bones of cattle and other animals bearing cur marks have been found at Sonpur, Khajuri, Narhan[26] and several other places. These belong to pre-NBPW times and to later periods. Numerous charred bones of cattle and other animals appear in Narhan.[27] Those from Pataliputra in the NBPW phase show the majority of the people to be meat eaters.[28]

The slaughter of cattle obstructed agriculture. The tribes who kept cattle and other animals for non-vegetarian food cannot be clearly identified though they lived in Anga, Magadha, Videha, Vajji, Kasi, Kosala and Vatsa. Many cattle were killed in Kasi and Kosala where Vedic sacrifices were performed. Early Buddhist texts including the *Suttanipāta* speak of Gautama Buddha's strong reaction against Vedic sacrifices[29] which suggests that important tribal chiefs of the mid-Ganga plains had imbibed Vedic culture. The chiefs were possibly heads of rural communities which used black-and-red ware, black slipped ware, red ware and other pre-NBP wares which occur at many excavated sites in the mid-Ganga basin. However, the needs of agriculture demanded the preservation of cattle wealth. Therefore, the earliest Buddhist texts teach that cows should not be killed because

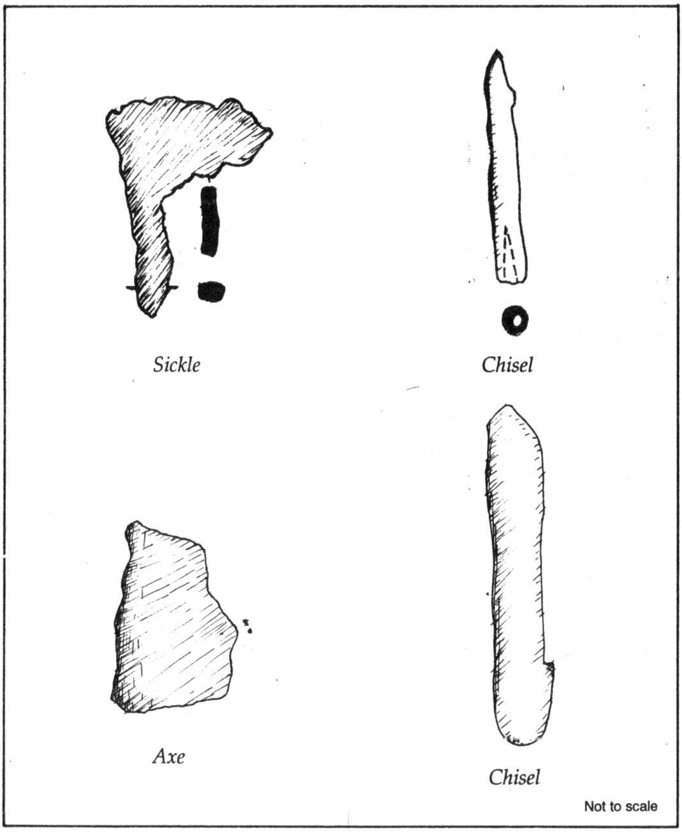

FIGURE 3: NBPW IRON AGRICULTURAL AND OTHER TOOLS FROM NARHAN AND SONPUR

they help in the growth of plants which confer food, beauty and happiness on the people. By the beginning of the Christian era the brahmanical texts also came to emphasise the virtues of not killing the cows[30], and added that the brahmana also should not be killed.

Revolution in Craft Production

Though craft specialisation can be traced back to neolithic-chalcolithic times, the second stage of iron brought about a major revolution in the production of craft goods. The production of low carbon steel led to the fabrication of more and more iron tools, which could be used to create various types of craft objects with greater ease and agility. The comparative table covering half a dozen sites (pp. 75-7) highlights the difference between the neolithic-chalcolithic phase and the Iron-NBPW phase at the same place in respect of craft goods.[31] This table shows that in the chalcolithic phase the total number of iron objects found at six sites is only 20 including a slag, whereas the total number of iron objects including a few slags at the same sites in the Iron-NBPW phase is 352.[32] Similarly at all the six sites the total number of copper objects is 22 in the chalcolithic phase but it rises to 175 in the post-chalcolithic phase.[33] The total number of bone objects at all the six sites except one in the neolithic-chalcolithic phase is 162 but goes up to 741 in the Iron-NBPW phase.[34] Similarly the number of semiprecious stone objects at these sites is 44 in the neolithic-chalcolithic phase but 169 in the Iron-NPBW phase.[35] The information about stone objects at these sites is scanty. They number 137 in the first phase and 250 in the second phase.[36] Ivory and glass goods also increase in number on account of the use of iron implements. The use of iron tools accounts for the find of numerous wooden logs and

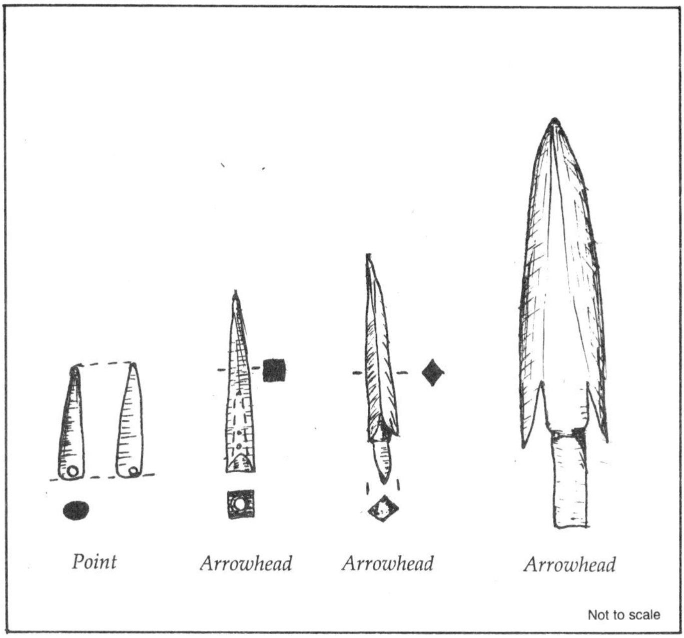

FIGURE 4: NBPW BONE AND COPPER TOOLS FROM NARHAN AND SONPUR

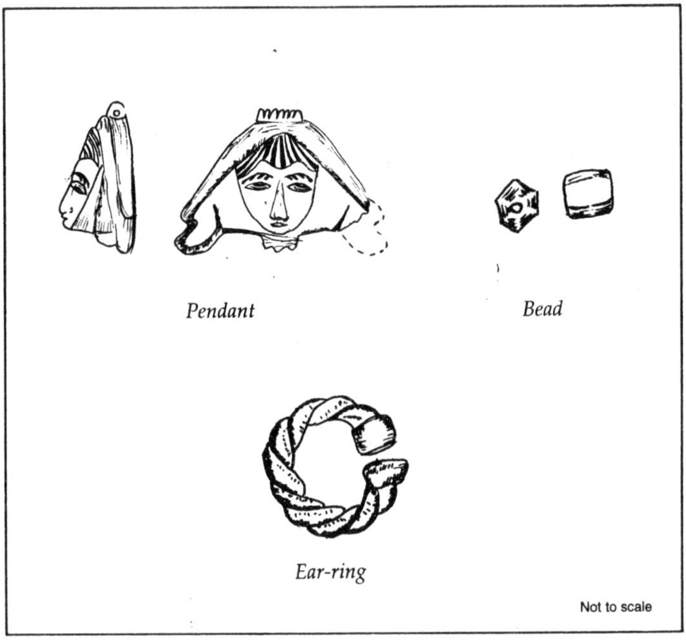

FIGURE 5: NBPW SEMIPRECIOUS STONE AND COPPER OBJECTS FROM SONPUR, ŚRĀVASTĪ AND VAISHALI

COMPARATIVE TABLE OF IRON AND OTHER RELATED CRAFT OBJECTS

	Neolithic - Chalcolithic									*Iron - NBPW*								
	Iron	Copper	Semiprecious Stone	Bone	Ivory	Shell	Coin	Glass	Stone	Iron	Copper	Semiprécious Stone	Bone	Ivory	Shell	Coin	Glass	Stone
CHIRAND[b] (1962-65 and 1696-71 excav. by Directorate of Archaeology & Museum, Govt. of Bihar, Patna. 1980-82 excav. by AIHA, Patna University	14	07	32	77	02	-	-	-	17	62	43	66[c]	420	08		80	15	07
KHAIRADIH (1980-81, 1981-82, 1985-86 & 1987-88 excav. by AIHCA, BHU)	-	02	-	-	-	-	-	-	-	31	23	-	-		-	09	-	-

	Iron	Copper	Semiprecious Stone	Bone	Ivory	Shell	Coin	Glass	Stone	Iron	Copper	Semiprecious Stone	Bone	Ivory	Shell	Coin	Glass	Stone
MANER (1984-85, 1986-89 & 1991-93 excav. by AIHA, P. U)	-	-	-	03	-	-	-	-	16	15	04	-	01	01	-	02	01	01
NARHAN (1984-89 excav. by AIHCA, BHU)	02	02	-	38	-	-	-	-	-	48	12	28	201	-	-	50[(d)]	27	-
Sonpur (1956 & 1959-62 excav. by Diretorate of Arhaeology & Museum, Govt. of Bihar, Patna	-	05	10	02	07	-	-	-	03	55	49	71	-	21	02	16	36	29

	Iron	Copper	Semiprecious Stone	Bone	Ivory	Shell	Coin	Glass	Stone	Iron	Copper	Semiprecious Stone	Bone	Ivory	Shell	Coin	Glass	Stone
TARADIH (1981-92 excav. by Directorate of Archaeology, Govt. of Bihar, Patna)	02	06	02	52	-	04	-	-	101	132	44	04	119	-	09	08	06	213

(a) Except for Sonpur this table has been prepared on the basis of Register of Antiquities supplied by B. S. Verma and B. Narayan for Chirand, B. P. Singh and Vibha Tripathi for Khairadih, B Narayan and A. K. Singh for Maner, Puroshottam Singh and A. K. Singh for Narhan, and A. K. Prasad for Taradih.

(b) In Chirand objects of horn are also included in the entry under Ivory.

(c) These entries are based on oral information supplied by B. S. Verma.

(d) Punch-marked coins are reported from the eroded section of the mound.

Abbrev: AIHA: Department of Ancient Indian History & Archaeology.
AIHCA: Department of Ancient Indian History, Culture and Archaeology.
excav.: Excavated.

palisades of *sāl* in the fourth century BC at several sites in Patna.[37] The *sāl* timber may have been obtained from the Chotanagpur plateau or the Himalayan terai. Polished Mauryan stone pillars could not appear without the use of iron tools. Even the manufacture of the NBPW, which is considered unique, may have benefited from the context in which iron technology thrived. Above all, the use of iron helped the advent of metal money. Coins, which are absent in the chalcolithic phase, appear in the NBPW phase in all the sites though in small quantities.[38] The use of metal money radically altered the mode of exchange, which in turn facilitated commodity production and long-distance trade.

This table does not include sites which are mainly known for the craft objects of only the NBPW phase and noted for the find of numerous artefacts made of iron and other material. Rajghat, Piprahwa-Ganwaria, Vaishali and Champa belong to this category. Of them the case of Ganwaria may be particularly noted. Here Period I shows only two pieces of iron lump and a share, but Period II identical with the NBPW phase shows as many as 21 iron tools which include ploughshares, scrappers, sickles, knives, rivetted plates, a horse bit and single specimen of arrowhead.[39] Similarly while Period I has 8 copper objects, Period II has 39 copper objects. Period II also shows 78 bone objects which are mainly bone points.[40] Further, Period I, i.e. the pre-NBPW phase, shows 9 glass bangles while Period II shows 75 fragments of glass bangles which are opaque.[41]

The enormous increase in production by artisans, which was due to the use of iron, is amply attested by the archaeological record. I have shown elsewhere that a good many iron objects belong to the early layers of the NBPW phase.[42] We need, however, more layerwise information on these and other objects. Taradih provides a good example.

According to its excavator Ajit Kumar Prasad, 21 iron object belong to the early level of the NBPW phase.[43] This pattern is more pronounced at Atranjikhera where 147 iron tools belong to the first phase of the NBPW period which is divided into four periods.[44] Altogether the existing evidence on the craft objects negates the view that no visible change occurred in material life till 300 BC.[45]

NOTES

1. The importance of iron in the clearance and settlement of the Ganga plains was underlined by D.D. Kosambi in his book *An Introduction to the Study of Indian History*, Popular Prakashan, Bombay, 1956, and other publications. I discussed this subject in some detail in my book *Material Culture and Social Formations in Ancient India*, Macmillan, Delhi, 1983.
2. *IAR 1984-85*, p. 77.
3. An iron ring attributed to the chalcolithic phase at Jhimjhimia (P.K. Chattopadhyaya, 'Archaeometallurgy in India: Studies in Tehnoculture in Early Copper and Iron Ages in Bihar and West Bengal', Ph.D. Thesis, Patna University, 1992) really belongs to the top layer of the NBPW phase (information from R.S. Singh, the excavator).
4. R.S. Sharma, op. cit., pp. 71-2. Three stages are suggested by Vibha Tripathi in her unpublished paper 'Iron Age in Uttar Pradesh Technolgical Innovation and Social Adaptation', but here we are concerned mainly with the first two stages.
5. N.C. Ghosh *et al.*, 'The Archaeological Background and Iron Sample from Hatigra', *Purātattva*, no. 18, 1987-8, pp. 21-7.
6. See Hatigra in Possehl, ed., 'Radiocarbon Dates for South Asian Archaeology' (unpublished), The University Museum, University of Pennsylvania, Philadelphia, June 1989.
7. H.C. Bhardwaj, 'Aspects of Early Technology in India', *Radiocarbon and Indian Archaeology*, ed., D.P. Agrawal and A. Ghosh, Bombay, 1973, p. 397. The view that in preindustrial times only low grade iron ores were used needs to be examined further.
8. I have benefited from discussions on this subject with Vibha Tripathi.

9. Kokalika Sutta.
10. P.K. Chattopadhyaya, op. cit.
11. B.P. Singh, 'Some Aspects of Life in Ancient Varanasi as revealed through the Archaeological Sources', Ph.D. Thesis, BHU, 1980.
12. *IAR 1985-86*, p. 8.
13. P. Singh *et al.*, *Bhāratī*, no. 3, 1985, p. 121.
14. *IAR 1982-83*, pp. 15-16.
15. B.P. Sinha and B.S. Verma, *Sonpur Excavations*, Patna, 1977, pp. 128-9.
16. Ibid., p. 128.
17. B.P. Sinha and L.A. Narain, *Pataliputra Exavations, 1955-56*, p. 55.
18. K.M. Srivastava's Report on Piprahwa—Ganwaria (unpublished), p. 385 (Courtesy: Archaeological Survey of India); K.M. Srivastava, *Discovery of Kapilavastu*, Books & Books, New Delhi, 1986, p. 230.
19. Srivastava, *Discovery of Kapilavastu*, p. 229.
20. R.S. Sharma, op. cit., p. 95.
21. B.P. Sinha and B.S. Verma, op. cit., p. 128.
22. *IAR 1985-86*, p. 122.
23. *Śatapatha Brāhmaṇa*, I.1.4.3; II. 5.3.4. However, in post-Vedic texts the transplanted variety is generally known as *śāli.*
24. R.S. Sharma, op. cit., Ch. VI.
25. B.P. Sinha and and B.S. Verma, op. cit., p. 7.
26. *IAR 1984-85*, p. 90.
27. Ibid.
28. B.P. Sinha and L.A. Narain, op. cit., p. 11.
29. See the Brāhmaṇadhammika Sutta.
30. Ibid.
31. See the table on pp. 75-7 of this book.
32. See table.
33. Ibid.
34. Ibid. This information does not include Khairadih.
35. Ibid.
36. See table.
37. L.A.W. Waddel, *Report on the Excavation at Patna*, Calcutta, 1903, pp. 22-3 and map, p. 45; J.A. Page, *Bulandibagh near Patna, ASI Report, 1926-27*, p. 135; cf. J.W. McCrindle, *Ancient India as Described by Megasthenes and Arrian*, rpt of 1877, London edn,

International Books and Periodicals Supply Service, Delhi, 1972, pp. 206-7, fn.

38. See table.
39. K.M. Srivastava, *Discovery of Kapilavastu,* Books & Books, New Delhi, 1986, pp. 229-30; Sirvastava's 'Report on Piprahwa-Ganwaria' (unpublished), p. 385f.
40. Ibid., p. 245.
41. Information from the unpublished report of Srivastava on Piprahwa-Ganwaria.
42. R.S. Sharma, op. cit., Appendices IV & V.
43. Written information in a tabular form.
44. R.C. Gaur, *Excavations at Atranjikhera,* Motilal Banarsidass, Delhi, 1983, p. 425.
45. Dilip. K. Chakravarti, 'Beginning of Iron and Social Change in India', *Indian Studies: Past and Present,* XIV, no. 4, 1973, 329-39; Chakravarti underplays the role of iron in his book *The Early Use of Iron in India,* OUP, Delhi, 1992.

CHAPTER 8

Surplus and Rise of the State and Stratified Society

Tools and Problems of Productivity

People often wonder, if iron is so important for civilization, why settlements did not occur near iron mines. Occasionally, tribals have practised iron smelting[1] near mines but the red soil, characteristic of such areas is not conducive to paddy farming. Even with fertilizers and irrigation, the paddy produced per acre in red soil is only half the yield in the Gangetic alluvium. Hence, no surplus could accrue from the use of iron tools in the red soil hilly area.

George Erdosy recognises the importance of iron in colonising the Gangetic plains and promoting agriculture, but he nevertheless questions its catalytic role in creating conditions for the rise of the state and cities in that area.[2] He attributes the production of surplus to the intensive use of the existing tools, gradual reduction of the fallow period through double cropping and other methods and to the demand for surplus by a stratified society.[3] But I did not notice any evidence of double cropping in alluvial tracts producing rice or wheat in the Bihar plains even in late 1920s or early 1930s. The paddy crop took seven to nine months to be ready, and in the remaining period only subsidiary crops could be raised.

At this point the distinction between cultivation of paddy through broadcasting and through transplantation in the context of the mid-Ganga plains should be taken note of. The first is confined to the low land areas while the second is suitable for comparatively upland areas free from water-logging. Further, paddy cultivation through broadcasting starts in February-March and comes to an end in December with the result that the land is under cropping for nearly ten months. In such a case double cropping is not possible. On the other hand, cultivation through transplantation takes only six months, and it is, therefore, possible to have a second crop. What is perhaps more important is that the yield from wet paddy production is one and a half to two and a half times the yield from broadcasting paddy seeds. Further, the cereals produced through transplantation are of a finer quality.

The intensive use of the existing tools in agriculture in the pre-Iron-NBPW phase[4] appears to be imaginary. The general absence of the digging tools and of the use of metals around 1000 BC[5] continues for a few centuries. The chalcolithic layers of Chirand, Maner, Sonpur, Taradih, Khairadih and Narhan show very few copper implements. The coppers count 7 at Chirand, 4 at Maner, 5 at Sonpur, 6 at Taradih, and 2 each at Khairadih and Narhan,[6] and none of them is shaped for digging the soil. And although stone implements in the neolithic-chalcolithic phase at these sites number only a few surprisingly Taradih shows a large number of them in that phase.[7] However, the number of bone implements found at these sites is considerable. In the neolithic-chalcolithic phase their number is 77 at Chirand, 3 at Maner, 2 at Sonpur, 52 at Taradih and 38 at Narhan.[8] Clearly in both the neolithic and chalcolithic stages agriculture was carried on with the help of bone tools. Antlers found in Chirand and Senuwar may have been used for digging. But we cannot visualise any substantial increase in production on the basis of their intensive use.

Most of the bone tools from Senuwar were points and used largely for hunting and skinning, and some were also employed in the preparation of hide and wood; only a solitary digging specimen from the chalcolithic phase has been found.[9] Numerous microliths of the chalcolithic phase are found. Their microwear examination discloses that they were generally used as simple piercing tools and also as arrowhead and spearhead.[10] So far there is no archaeological evidence suggesting an intensive use of tools for agricultural purposes.

Social Differentiation

Ethnographic examples from eastern India may throw some light on the nature of social formation in the neolithic-chalcolithic phase. In the case of the Lushais (Mizos), know-ledgeable farmers were asked to locate suitable lands for *jhum* cultivation.[11] Those who succeeded were allowed the first choice of cultivating the fields.[12] Such distinctions in the distribution of land may have emerged in the chalcolithic phase. Use of beads of semiprecious stones as prestige objects appear as indicators of some social differentiation, which can also be inferred from some differences in various types of chalcolithic pottery.

Though such a differentiation had started in chalcolithic society in the plains, more of it can be inferred from the artefacts of NBPW/Iron times. Arrowheads and spearheads, which indicate the coercive power of the state, seem to have been confined to the chief and their kinsman and supporters. Different types of ware clearly indicate hierarchical social groups. The NBPW and black slipped ware and possibly the grey ware were meant for use by the upper classes comprising priests, warriors, state officials, monks and rich traders while the red ware and black-and-red ware served the needs of the peasants, artisans and other members of lower orders. Some social differentiation can also be inferred from terracotta objects.

Structural differences are far more important for the study of social differentiation, but they cannot be identified in the mid-Ganga plains in the pre-brick age for want of available structures. We have mud ramparts at half a dozen places, but very few mud dwellings have been discovered so far. Settlement sizes noticed on the periphery of the plains may not mean much in terms of social differentiation.

Problem of Dating

The origin of the state and stratified society in the mid-Ganga basin cannot be dated prior to the use of iron in agricultural production.[13] The Buddhist and brahmanical texts dealing with this area are not older than *c.* 500 BC, and they show that regular taxes and professional army, the two essential organs of the territorial state, did not appear until the date.[14] The existing archaeological evidence makes it difficult to ascribe the rise of the states in Kosala and Magadha to *c.* 600 BC. The calibrated radiocarbon dates provided by M. Stüiver give 400 BC for Ayodhya, 406 BC for Kausambi, 391 BC for Piprahwa and 400 BC for Rajghat for the NBPW.[15] For Manjhi in Saran district the calibrated radiocarbon date is 400 BC.[16] There is no doubt that the NBPW was the most distinctive pottery of the Iron Age society in the mid-Ganga plains. While many samples meant for radiocarbon dating belong to the mid-levels of the NBPW[17], others from the mid-Ganga sites belong to the early levels. Hence, on the basis of pre-mid-level deposits these dates can be pushed back to *c.* 500 BC,[18] which may be the starting point for social stratification and the early state.

The State and Social Inequality

According to the Dharmaśāstras the primary duty of the king or the head of the state is to uphold the institutions of family, property and, more importantly, the hierarchical varna system. These texts do not refer to territorial inequality. Work done on settlement archaeology in the western peripheries of the mid-Ganga plains[19] underlines the unequal sizes of settlements. But irrespective of their sizes privileged interest groups appear in those settlements which employ advanced means of production. It is these interest groups which play the main role in the formation of the state and stratified society. Therefore, even the earliest law-books enjoin the head of the state to uphold the varna system, which was based on inequality of power, status and resources. They do not require the king to maintain inequality of size between settled tracts, though chiefs of larger settlements may have subjugated those of the smaller ones. At any rate how social differentiation is linked to settlement sizes in the mid-Ganga plains needs to be worked out. The finding that large nucleated villages appeared in the doab area of Allahabad district in 1000-600 BC[20] is confined to two tiered settlement hierarchy and suggests a simple political structure.[21]

The real distinction between settlements appears with the construction of forts in the mid-Ganga plains around 500 BC. The artefacts from the fort areas suggest social differentiation. Ancient Indian texts regard fort as one of the seven elements of the state. It signifies the use and concentration of force at selected places. *Durga,* the term used for fort, indicates the fortified capital which formed the headquarters of the army. The existence of the states in the mid-Ganga plains is confirmed by the presence of forts at Champa, Rajgir and Sravasti. Except Rajgir the other two forts had mud ramparts which have been exposed through digging. Since NBPW occurs in the fort sites they seem to belong to *c.* 500 BC.[22] A good number of iron arrowheads, spearheads, lances, axes, blades or knife blades, etc., which may have been used by the soldiers, should be taken note of. Terracotta sling balls which appear in large numbers may have also been used in fighting.

Beginnings of Fortification and Urbanisation

Though it might be difficult to postulate how the forts originated in the mid-Ganga plains, nevertheless excavations at Kankarbagh provide conclusive evidence of the earliest enclosed settlement. The earliest trace of an enclosed settlement has been found at Kankarbagh. The wooden palisades, discovered there in the course of digging for drainage, carry calibrated dates ranging from 720 BC to 550 BC. Of the seven such dates one belongs to the first quarter of the eighth century BC, three dates to the seventh century BC, and the remaining three to the first half of the sixth century BC, the last stopping at 550 BC.[23] These wooden logs, which number thirteen and in their present condition range in height from 3 m 49 cm to 2 m 16 cm,[24] suggest fenced settlements, which may have been used by smaller chiefs or the village community for their defence. In any

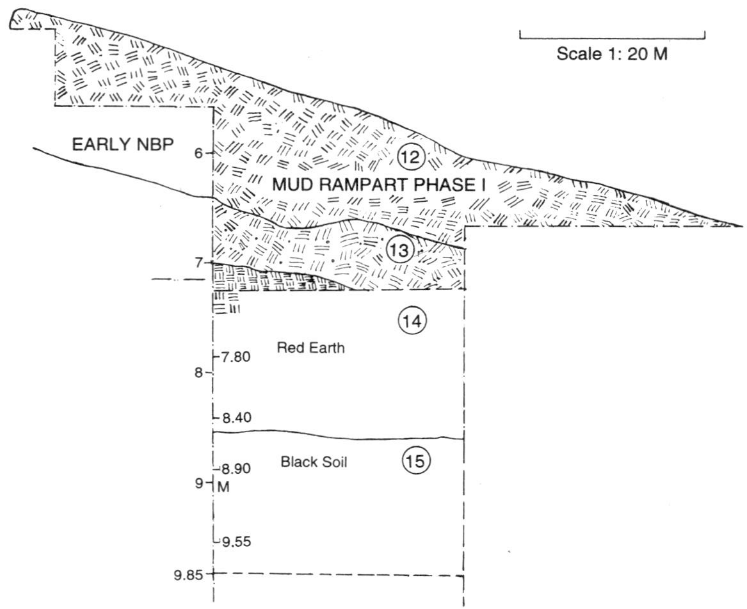

FIGURE 6: EARLY NBPW MUD FORT AT CHAMPA (SECTION LOOKING NORTH)

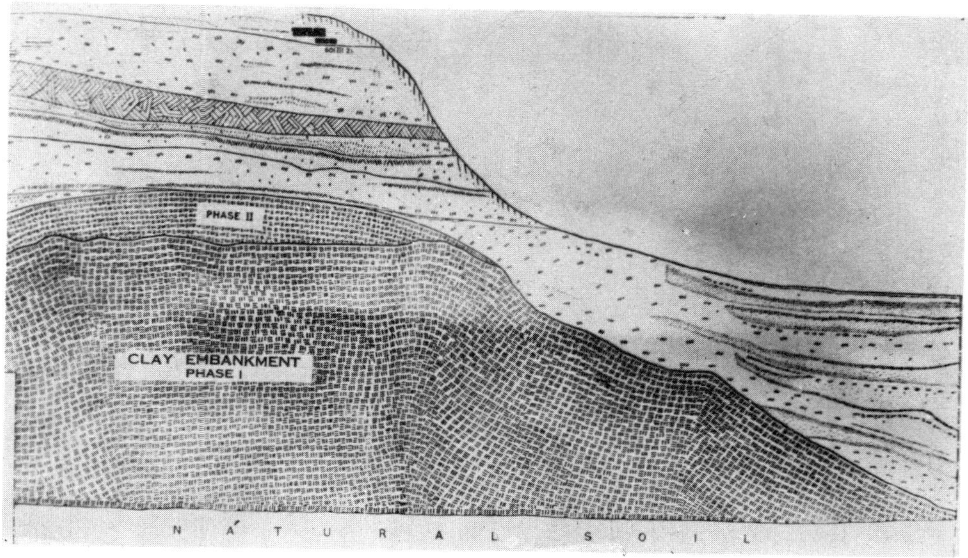

FIGURE 7: EARLY NBPW MUD EMBANKMENT AT RAJGHAT

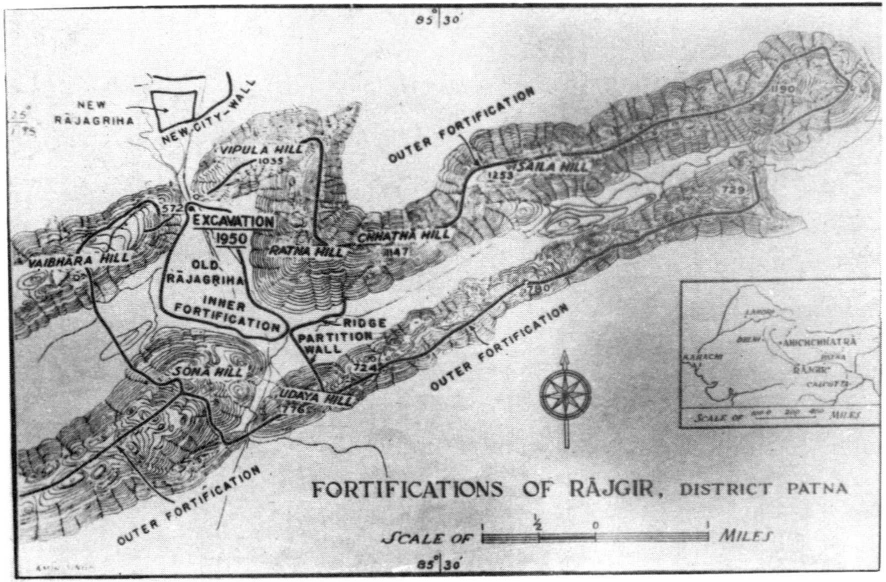

PLATE 4: EARLY NBPW FORTIFICATION AT RAJGIR *(Courtesy: ASI)*

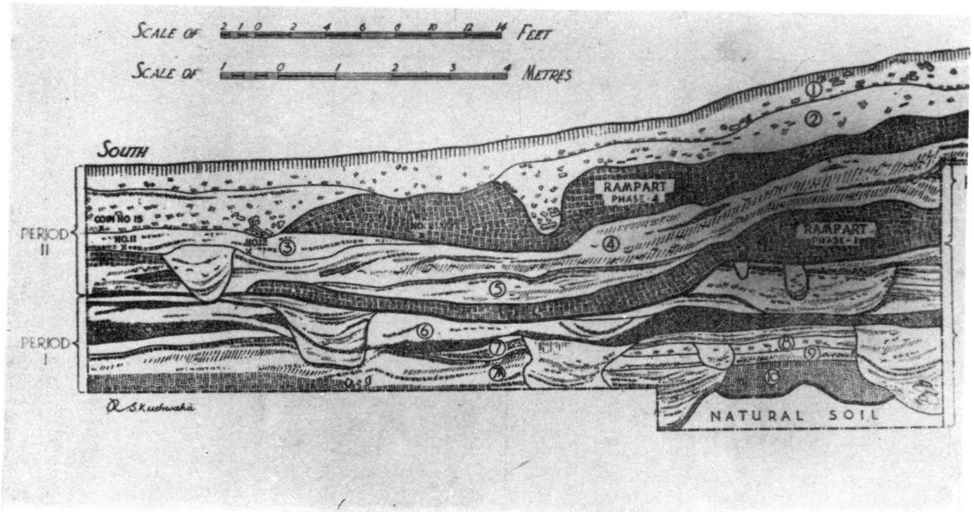

FIGURE 8: EARLY NBPW MUD FORT AT ŚRĀVASTĪ *(Courtesy: Banaras Hindu University)*

case the fort may be considered a culmination of the process which had started with wooden enclosure. In his *Indika* Megasthenes mentions the palisades of Pataliputra. It should however be noted that both the ramparts and the palisades suggest the use of iron tools used for deep digging and cutting.

In the pre-NBPW period iron weapons may have added to the power of the chief but could not convert chiefdom into a state. The breakthrough came only with the use of iron in agriculture and crafts which ensured taxes for maintaining the warriors or kṣatriyas and gifts for supporting the priests. Once the state was firmly established it could compel the peasants to produce surplus, as is evident from the provision for emergency taxation in the *kośābhisaṃharaṇam* section of the *Arthaśāstra* of Kauṭilya.[25] The process of surplus strengthening the state and the state forcing the peasants to produce surplus went on unabated in ancient India.

The role of iron in the rise of cities has often been questioned and the main credit is given to the state.[26] There is no doubt that the *durgavidhāna*[27] and *durganiveśa*[28] sections of the *Arthaśāstra* of Kauṭilya enjoin the king to found walled town just as he is asked to found villages in the *janapadaniveśa*[29] section. Even so, it is difficult to visualize the rise of either the city or the state in the mid-Ganga plains without high productivity made possible by iron tools. If it is to be believed that the state is based on privileged interest groups living on gifts, taxes and tributes, can the substantial increase in production and settlements be ruled out, and can this increase occur in the thickly forested and hard alluvium soil area without the use of iron tools? The view that the chalcolithic tools could produce surplus in the mid-Ganga basin is unrealistic.

Both the state and urbanism appear around 500 BC. But urbanisation is not essential to the formation of the early state.[30] In a table given by Claessen as many as twenty-one early states are analysed from this and other angles, and only twelve of them show evidence of urbanisation.[31] Childe and Adams suggested urbanisation as a characteristic of the early state[32] obviously on the basis of their studies of the Bronze Age cultures. While this is not universally true[33] the view that the state promotes urbanisation is plausible.

Urbanisation in the mid-Ganga plains is different from its Harappan counterpart,[34] and appears in two stages. Its first stage begins with *c.* 500 BC and shows craft objects, coins, trade, mud buildings, etc. The second stage appears in *c.* 300 BC and shows mature urbanisation distinguished by the coming of ring wells, soakpits, brick structures, writing, etc. A. Ghosh speaks of the beginning of the genuine towns from about 300 BC onwards.[35] These mature towns may have been set up by the early state.

The states of 'North India and Pakistan at the time of the Buddha' cannot be called city states, a label applied to them by Erdosy.[36] The concept of 'city state', which is used in ancient Greek history, means that a city forms an independent state. This is not so in north India where such states, issuing their own coins, appear only in post-Maurya times.

Archaeology and Gautama Buddha

I have not been able to see all the arguments for placing Gautama Buddha in the fourth century BC or later.[37] But enamoured of the Harappan bricks and wedded to the idea of monumental buildings being characteristics of towns, some archaeologists find it difficult to swallow the possibility of state formation or city formation in the pre-brick stage in the mid-Ganga plains. Their difficulty is compounded by non-discovery of mud buildings in over two dozen excavated sites in this area. Mud ramparts and stupas have been exposed at several sites, but except for a mud wall reported from Ganwaria in Basti district and a mud-brick wall from Khairadih in Ballia district, no other mud buildings have been reported from any mid-Ganga site. It is difficult to say whether the paucity of the finds is due to lack of archaeological skill and the primitive methods used or due to the weather conditions which are marked by humidity, heavy showers and frequent floods prevalent in this area. However even the age of mud structures is marked by the use of metal money, semiprecious stones, gold jewellery, glass objects, iron tools and weapons, highly polished pottery, ivory and fortified settlements. These certainly indicate social differentiation, and formation of states and cities. The material culture of the Pali texts of pre-Maurya times broadly corresponds to the Iron/NBPW archaeology of Kosala and Magadha.

It would be as wrong to attribute all the Buddhist teachings to Gautama Buddha as to attribute all the Platonic ideas and teachings to Plato. It is well known that many teachings of his disciples were fathered on Plato. The same may also be said of the Buddha. On the basis of style and contents the Pali texts show stratification which has not been satisfactorily settled except in the case of the *Suttanipāta*. Therefore, the date of the Buddha does not depend entirely on the teachings attributed to him in the Buddhist texts. Dates based purely on literary traditions do require rethinking. Texts aided and supported by archaeology are certainly preferable, but the archaeology of the mid-Ganga plains deserves more scientific attention than it has received.

NOTES

1. This question was raised in several university seminars where I spoke on the problem of iron.

2. George Erdosy, *Urbanisation in Early Historic India*, BAR International Series, 430, Oxford, 1988, pp. 112, 125-7.
3. Ibid., pp. 127-9.
4. Op. cit., pp. 127-9.
5. Ibid., p. 128.
6. See table.
7. Ibid.
8. Ibid.
9. B.P. Singh, 'Evidence of Utilisation of Bones at Senuwar', in *Bhāratī*, vol. 20, 1993-4, pp. 55-7.
10. Gayatri Chaturvedi, 'Functional analysis of microlithic points', *Bhāratī*, vol. 20, 1993-4, pp. 111-12.
11. N.E. Perry, *A Monograph on Lushai Customs and Ceremonies*, Aizwal, 1973, pp. 7-8.
12. cf. Ibid.
13. R.S. Sharma, *Origin of the State in India*, University of Bombay, 1989.
14. Ibid; cf. Romila Thapar, *From Lineage to the State*, OUP, Delhi, 1984.
15. Gregory L. Possehl, 'Radiocarbon Dates for South Asian Archaeology', University Museum, University of Pennsylvania, Philadelphia, 1989 (unpublished), Calib-2 on pp. 4, 27-8 and 41-2.
16. George Erdosy in F. R. Allchin with contributions from others, *The Archaeology of Early Historic South Asia*, CUP, 1995, p. 103.
17. Makkhan Lal, 'Chronology of the Protohistoric and Early Historic Culture of the Upper Ganga Plains', in *East and West*, vol. 30, nos. 1-3, 1986, pp. 13-100.
18. The NBPW in general is dated between 700 and 100 BC (ibid.), but in the context of the mid-Ganga plains it is reasonable to place the beginning of the NBPW in *c.* 500 BC (Vibha Tripathi, 'Early Historic Archaeology and Radiocarbon Dating' in *The Indian Historical Review*, vol. XIV, nos. 1-2, pp. 20-5).
19. Makkhan Lal, *Settlement History and Rise of Civilization in Ganga-Yamuna Doab from 1500 BC-300 AD*, Delhi, 1984; Erdosy, *Urbanisation in Early Historic India*.
20. Erdosy, ibid., p. 127.
21. Erdosy in F.R. Allchin, op. cit., p. 81.
22. Rajghat and Vaishali do not have early NBPW mud forts, though the mud embankment at Rajghat suggests the

construction of mud ramparts around 500 BC. The dates of forts at Rajgir and Champa are not earlier than 500 BC, as shown by Erdosy, ibid., pp. 109-10.

23. Gregory L. Possehl, 'Radiocarbon Dates for South Asian Archaeology', University of Pennsylvania, Philadelphia, 1989 (unpublished), p. 26. Calib-2.
24. They are in the custody of Patna Museum.
25. *The Kauṭilīya Arthaśāstra*, pt. I, University of Bombay, 1960, V. 2.
26. A. Ghosh, *The City in Early Historical India*, Indian Institute of Advanced Study, Simla, 1973.
27. *The Kauṭilīya Arthaśāstra*, pt. I, ed. R.P. Kangle, University of Bombay, 1960, II. 3.
28. Ibid., II. 4.
29. Ibid., II. 1.
30. Hermann Kulke thinks that urbanisation preceded the process of genuine state formation by some generations, 'Some Considerations on the Significance of Buddha's Date for History of North India', Heinz Bechert, ed., *The Dating of the Historical Buddha*, Göttingen, 1991, pt. I, pp. 100-7 (p. 106).
31. Henri J.M. Claessen and Peter Skalnik, eds., *The Early State*, Mouton Publishers, The Hague, 1978.
32. Ibid., p. 541.
33. Ibid.
34. R.S. Sharma, *Perspectives in Social and Economic History of Early India*, Munshiram Manoharlal, New Delhi, 1995, pp. 201-3.
35. A. Ghosh, op. cit.
36. Erdosy in F.R. Allchin, op. cit., p. 99.
37. Some of these appear in Hermann Kulke, 'Some Considerations on the Significance of Buddha's Date for the History of North India' in Heinz Bechert, ed., *The Dating of the Historical Buddha*, Vandenhoeck and Rupreht, Göttingen, 1991, pp. 100-7.

Summing-up

It is difficult to make archaeological material meaningful without ideological awareness. Diffusionism attributes developments to external factors and processualism to local factors. But if it is not backed by archaeological data diffusionism degenerates into colonialism, and in a similar situation processualism shades off into fundamentalism and feeds the myth about the uniqueness and greatness of indigenous cultures. Even at the local level the role of artefacts canot be critically appreciated without reference to changes in technology, the quality and availability of the raw material, the types of climate and soil in which they were used and the conditions which determined their survival.

Indication of some kind of chieftainship and social

differentiation can be inferred from the neolithic-chalcolithic phase. But the real transformation took place in the second stage of the use of iron which acted as a catalyst in material life. The iron using people of the mid-Ganga plains enlarged the settlements area enormously. They went far ahead of their predecessors in respect of artifactual equipment, commercial and artisanal activities, and agricultural production. Whether advanced iron technology came from the west to the east is debatable. But the eastward progress of the PGW and its close connection with the black slipped ware and the NBPW is difficult to deny. Glass also travelled eastward. So also was the case with the use of horse and spoked wheel which revolutionised war and mode of transport, and strengthened the ruling groups. Migration to the east is also suggested by the spread of mortuary practices and Indo-Aryan language. All this created conditions suitable for the formation of the state and complex society. Communication through writing and the Indo-Aryan language unified the ruling class and helped its integration with the people. Metal money and a common speech over a wide area facilitated exchange of goods and skills, and promoted inter-tribe and inter-group contacts.

Though the neolithic-chalcolithic people provided basic elements of craft and agriculture, high productivity and fairly populated settlements appeared as a result of interaction with the later Vedic people. Therefore, the mid-Ganga state and varna society were the ultimate outcome of the development of the Iron-NBPW cultures.

Bibliography

Allchin, F.R. with contributions from George Erdosy, R.A.E. Conningham, D.K. Chakravarti and Bridget Allchin, *The Archaeology of Early Historic South Asia: The Emergence of Cities and States*, Cambridge University Press, 1995.

Atharvaveda Saṃhitā (School of the Śaunakas), ed., C.R. Lanman, tr., W.D. Whitney, Harvard Oriental Series, Harvard University, 1905.

Banerjea, A.C., *Studies in the Brāhmaṇas*, Motilal Banarsidass, Delhi, 1963.

Bechert, Heinz, ed., *When did the Buddha live? The Controversy on the Dating of the Historical Buddha*, Sri Satguru Publications, Delhi, 1995.

Bhardwaj, H.C. 'Aspects of Early Technology in India' in D.P.

Agrawal and A. Ghosh, eds, *Radiocarbon and Indian Archaeology*, Tata Institute of Fundamental Research, Bombay, 1973.

Chakravarti, Dilip K. 'Beginning of Iron and Social Change in India' in *Indian Studies: Past and Present*, xiv, no. 4, 1973.

———, *The Early Use of Iron in India*, Oxford University Press, Delhi, 1992.

Chattopadhyaya, K.P., *The Ancient Indian Culture Contacts and Migrations*, Calcutta, 1970.

Chattopadhyaya, P.K. 'Archaeometallurgy in India: Studies in Technoculture in Early Copper and Iron Ages in Bihar and West Bengal', Ph.D. Thesis, Patna University, Patna, 1992.

Chattopadhyaya, U.C., 'Report on Faunal Remains in Narhan' in Purushottam Singh, *Excavations at Narhan (1984-89)*, Banaras Hindu University and D.K. Publishers, Delhi, 1994.

Chaturvedi, Gayatri, 'Functional analysis of microlithic points' in *Bhāratī*, vol. 20, 1993-4.

Chaturvedi, S.N., 'Advance of Vindhyan Neolithic and Chalcolithic Cultures to the Himalayan Terai' in *Man and Environment*, IX, 1985.

Claessen, Henri J.M. and Peter Skalnik, eds, *The Early State*, Mouton Publishers, The Hague, 1978.

Dev, Krishna and Vijayakant Mishra, *Vaishali Excavations: 1950*, Vaishali Sangh, Vaishali, 1961.

Erdosy, George, *Urbanisation in Early Historic India*, BAR International Series, 430, Oxford, 1988.

Gaur, R.C. *Excavations at Atranjikhera*, Motilal Banarsidass, Delhi, 1983.

Ghosh, A., *The City in Early Historical India*, Indian Institute of Advanced Study, Simla, 1973.

Gosh, A., ed., *An Encyclopaedia of Indian Archaeology*, 2 vols., Munshiram Manoharlal, New Delhi, 1989.

Indian Archaeology—A Review, 1971-72, 1978-79, 1981-82, 1982-83, 1983-84, 1984-85 and *1985-86*, Archaeological Survey of India, New Delhi.

Kauṭilīya Arthaśāstra, ed. & tr., R.P. Kangle, vols. I & II, University of Bombay, Bombay, 1960.

Ghosh, N.C. *et al.*, 'The Archaeological Background and Iron

Sample from Hatigra', in *Purātattva*, no. 18, 1987-8.

Grignard, A., S.J. *Hahn's Oraon Folk-lore in the Original: A critical text with translations and notes,* Government Printing, Bihar and Orissa, Gulzarbagh, Patna, 1931.

Joshi, Jagat Pati, *Excavation at Bhagwanpura 1975-76 and Other Explorations & Excavations 1975-81 in Haryana, Jammu and Kashmir and Punjab,* Archaeological Survey of India, New Delhi, 1993.

Kennedy, Kenneth A.R. *et al.*, 'Mesolithic Human Remains from the Gangetic Plain: Sarai Nehar Rai' in *Purātattva,* no. 15, 1984-5.

Kosambi, D.D., *An Introduction to the Study of Indian History*, Popular Prakashan, Bombay, 1956.

———, *The Culture and Civilization of Ancient India in Historical Outline,* Routeledge and Kegan Paul, London, 1965.

Kulke, Hermann, 'Some Considerations on the Significance of Buddha's Date for the History of North India' in Heinz Bechert, ed., *The Dating of the Historical Buddha,* Vandenhoeck and Rupreht, Göttingen, 1991.

Kumar, Ravindra, 'Archaeology of the Middel Gomati Basin with special reference to Sultanpur District, U.P.' Ph.D. Thesis, BHU, 1990.

Lal, B.B., 'Painted Grey Ware Culture of the Iron Age' in A.H. Dani and V.M. Masson, eds., *A History of Civilizations of Central Asia*, vol. I, The dawn of civilization: Earliest times to 700 BC, UNESCO Publishing, Paris, 1992.

Lal, Makkhan, *Settlement History and Rise of Civilization in Ganga-Yamuna Doab from 1500 BC -300 AD,* B.R. Publishing House, Delhi, 1984.

———, 'Chronology of the Protohistoric and Early Historic Cultures of the Upper Ganga Plains' in *East and West,* vol. 36, nos. 1-3, September 1986.

Macdonell, A.A. and A.B. Keith, *Vedic Index of Names and Subjects*, 2 vols., Motilal Banarsidass, Delhi, rpt, 1967.

Malalasekera, G.P., *Dictionary of Pāli Proper Names*, rpt, The Pali Text Society, London, 1974.

McCrindle, J.W., *Ancient India as Described by Megasthenes and*

Arrian, rpt of 1877, London edn, International Books and Periodicals Supply Service, Delhi, 1972.

Mishra, Yogendra, *An Early History of Vaiśāli*, Motilal Banarsidass, Delhi, 1962.

Misra, A.K., 'Ganga Valley: Twilights on its Problems as revealed in Archaeological Excavations' in *Prāgdhārā*, no. 1, 1990-1.

Narain, A.K. and T.N. Roy, *The Excavations at Prahladpur, March-April, 1963*, BHU, Varanasi, 1968.

———, *Excavations at Rajghat*, pt. II, BHU, Varanasi, 1977.

Narayan, Basudev, *Prehistoric Archaeology of Bihar*, K.P. Jayaswal Research Institute, Patna, 1996.

Page, J.A., *Bulandibagh near Patna*, Archaeological Survey of India Report, 1926-7.

Pañcaviṃśa Brāhmaṇa, tr., W. Caland, Bibliotheca Indica, Calcutta, 1931.

Pargiter, F.E. *Ancient Indian Historical Traditions*, London, 1922.

Patil, D.R., *Antiquarian Remains in Bihar*, K.P. Jayaswal Research Institute, Patna, 1963.

Peppe, W.C. and V.A. Smith, 'The Piprahwa Stupa containing Relics of Buddha' in *JASB*, 1898.

Perry, N.E., *A Monograph on Lushai Customs and Ceremonies*, Aizwal, 1973.

Possehl, Gregory L., 'Radiocarbon Dates for South Asian Archaeology', University Museum, University of Pennsylvania, Philadelphia, June 1989 (unpublished).

Possehl, Gregory, L. and Paul C. Rissman, *India* in Robert W. Ehrichs, ed., *Chronologies in Old World Archaeology*, vol. I, University of Chicago Press, Chicago, 1992.

Raychaudhuri, H.C., *Political History of Ancient India*, 7th edn, University of Calcutta, Calcutta, 1972.

Rhys Davids, T.W. and W. Stede, *Pali-English Dictionary*, PTS, London, 1921.

Roy, T.N. *The Ganges Civilization*, Ramanand Vidya Bhawan, New Delhi, 1983.

Saraswat, K.S., 'Seed and Fruit Remains of Imlidih-Khurd, Gorakhpur: A Preliminary Report' in *Prāgdhārā*, no. 3, (1933).

Śatapatha Brāhmaṇa (Mādhyandina) recension, ed., V. Sharma

Gauda and C.D. Sharma, Kasi, Saṃvat 1894-7.

Sharma, R.S., *Some Economic Aspects of the Caste System in Ancient India,* Patna, 1952.

———, *Material Culture and Social Formations in Ancient India,* Macmillan, Delhi, 1983.

———, *Perspectives in Social and Economic History of Early India,* 2nd edn, Munshiram Manoharlal, New Delhi, 1995.

———, *Origin of the State in India,* Department of History, University of Bombay, Bombay, 1989.

———, *Śūdras in Ancient India,* 3rd edn, Motilal Banarsidass, Delhi, 1990.

———, *Aspects of Political Ideas and Institutions in Ancient India,* 3rd edn, Motilal Banarsidass, Delhi, 1991.

Sharma, G.R. *et al., Beginning of Agriculture,* Abinash Prakashan, Allahabad, 1980.

Singh, B.P. 'Some Aspects of Life in Ancient Varanasi as revealed through Archaeological Sources', Ph.D. Thesis, BHU, 1980.

———, 'Evidence for Utilisation of Bones at Senuwar' in *Bhāratī,* vol. 20, 1993-4.

Singh, P. and M. Lal, 'Narhan, 1983-85: 'A Preliminary Report of Archaeological Excavations' in *Bhāratī,* NS., no. 3, Varanasi, 1985.

Singh, P. *et al.*, 'Explorations along the Kuwana River in Districts of Gorakhpur and Basti' in *Prāgdhārā,* no. 1, 1990-1.

Singh, Purushottam, *Excavations at Narhan (1984-9)*, BHU and D.K. Publishers, Delhi, 1994.

Sinha, B.P. and S.R. Roy, *Vaiśālī Excavations, 1958-62,* Directorate of Archaeology and Museums, Bihar, Patna, 1969.

Sinha, B.P. and B.S. Verma, *Sonpur Excavations (1956 and 1959-62)*, Directorate of Archaeology and Museums, Bihar, Patna, 1977.

Sinha, B.P. and L.A. Narain, *Pataliputra Excavations 1955-56,* Directorate of Archaeology and Museums, Bihar, Patna, 1970.

Sinha, C.P. and B.K. Chaudhary, 'Excavations at Hajipur', *The Journal of the Bihar Purāvid Pariṣad,* vols. XI and XII (Prof. Yogendra Mishra Commemoration Volume), 1987-8, pp. 256-60.

Srivastava, K.M. *Discovery of Kapilavastu*, Books & Books, New Delhi, 1986.

Spate, O.H.K. and A.T.H. Learmonth, *India and Pakistan: A General and Regional Geography*, Methuen & Co. Ltd., London, 1967.

Thapar, Romila, *From Lineage to the State*, Oxford University Press, Delhi, 1984.

Tripathi, Vibha, 'Early Historic Archaeology and Radiocarbon Dating' in *The Indian Historical Review*, vol. XIV, nos. 1-2.

———, 'A Micro-Level Study of Painted Grey Ware Culture' in *Prāgdhārā*, no. 1, 1990-91.

———, 'Iron Age in Uttar Pradesh—Technological Innovation and Social Adaptation' (unpublished).

Waddel, L.A.W., *Report on the Excavation at Patna*, Calcutta, 1903.

Index